Cambridge Elements ☰

Elements in Contentious Politics
edited by
David S. Meyer
University of California, Irvine
Suzanne Staggenborg
University of Pittsburgh

PROTEST AND POLICY IN THE IRAQ, NUCLEAR FREEZE AND VIETNAM PEACE MOVEMENTS

David Cortright
University of Notre Dame

CAMBRIDGE
UNIVERSITY PRESS

CAMBRIDGE
UNIVERSITY PRESS

Shaftesbury Road, Cambridge CB2 8EA, United Kingdom

One Liberty Plaza, 20th Floor, New York, NY 10006, USA

477 Williamstown Road, Port Melbourne, VIC 3207, Australia

314–321, 3rd Floor, Plot 3, Splendor Forum, Jasola District Centre,
New Delhi – 110025, India

103 Penang Road, #05–06/07, Visioncrest Commercial, Singapore 238467

Cambridge University Press is part of Cambridge University Press & Assessment,
a department of the University of Cambridge.

We share the University's mission to contribute to society through the pursuit of
education, learning and research at the highest international levels of excellence.

www.cambridge.org
Information on this title: www.cambridge.org/9781009640282

DOI: 10.1017/9781009640275

First published 2025

A catalogue record for this publication is available from the British Library

ISBN 978-1-009-64028-2 Hardback
ISBN 978-1-009-64024-4 Paperback
ISSN 2633-3570 (online)
ISSN 2633-3562 (print)

Cambridge University Press & Assessment has no responsibility for the persistence
or accuracy of URLs for external or third-party internet websites referred to in this
publication and does not guarantee that any content on such websites is, or will remain,
accurate or appropriate.

For EU product safety concerns, contact us at Calle de José Abascal, 56, 1°, 28003
Madrid, Spain, or email eugpsr@cambridge.org

Protest and Policy in the Iraq, Nuclear Freeze and Vietnam Peace Movements

Elements in Contentious Politics

DOI: 10.1017/9781009640275
First published online: May 2025

David Cortright
University of Notre Dame
Author for correspondence: David Cortright, dcortrig@nd.edu

Abstract: This Element addresses questions about social movement effectiveness and the strategies and methods that are most likely to achieve policy change. It examines the nature of peace movements through a comparative analysis of three major movements, focusing on their policy impacts. It assesses social movement dynamics and the mechanisms through which movements gain influence. The purpose is to mine campaign experiences from the past to develop action guidelines for more effective citizen activism against war and nuclear weapons in the future. The Element examines non-institutional and institutional forms of politics and the relationship between the two, and how they can be mutually reinforcing. It traces examples of inside–outside approaches within the three peace movements and their effects. Lessons from the analysis and case studies are applied in the final section to proposals for a new global freeze movement to stop the emerging international arms race.

Keywords: peace, nuclear, movement, antiwar, policy

ISBNs: 9781009640282 (HB), 9781009640244 (PB), 9781009640275 (OC)
ISSNs: 2633-3570 (online), 2633-3562 (print)

Contents

1 Introduction

In December 2011, as the last US troops were leaving Iraq, I received a phone call from the White House. It was the first and only time I've been called by the White House. On the line that day was the director of the Office of Public Engagement, a small bureau created by the Obama administration as a means of exchanging views with civil society groups. "We just want to say thank you," the director of the office said, "to you and other activists in the antiwar movement. What the President accomplished today would not have been possible without the work you and so many did over the past few years." He was calling because of my role in helping to create Win Without War, a national network opposed to the invasion and occupation of Iraq. I was speechless and humbled, and grateful to realize that what he said was probably true. We, the global antiwar movement of tens of millions of people, had resisted the invasion on an unprecedented scale. In the United States we organized politically to turn Congress against the occupation and helped to elect a president who promised to withdraw the troops and was now fulfilling that pledge. It felt like a rare moment of success for the peace movement.

Few activists paid much attention to the withdrawal from Iraq and no celebrations were organized. The mood among activists was solemn, with sadness at the immense loss of life caused by the war and regret that they had not been able to stop the invasion in 2003. Few recognized their hand in helping to change US policy and end the occupation.

That episode reminded me of a similar experience in 1987 when I was invited to a conference by the Green Party in Germany to evaluate the recently signed treaty eliminating intermediate-range nuclear forces (INF) in Europe. The German Greens and European disarmament movement had battled NATO and Warsaw Pact missiles for a decade, organizing in the early 1980s the largest peace demonstrations in modern European history. NATO officials ignored the protests and proceeded with the deployment of the new missiles in 1983. Now they were signing a treaty with the Soviet Union to eliminate all of them. They were enacting the zero option that the movement had demanded. The placards carried through the streets of London and Bonn had read "no to Cruise and Pershing, no to SS-20," protesting both NATO and Soviet missiles.

The Greens were unexpectedly glum and uncertain about how to interpret the landmark INF treaty. Because the movement had failed to prevent the initial NATO deployment, activists believed their struggle had been a failure. The surprisingly positive agreement was not anticipated but was certainly welcome. I told the gathering we should celebrate the treaty and claim it as our own. We may have lost the battle against initial deployment, but we won the larger struggle to rid Europe of these menacing missiles.

The difficulty of recognizing success was present during the Vietnam antiwar movement as well. I experienced this as an active-duty soldier opposed to the war while stationed at Ft. Wadsworth, New York. Dozens of fellow soldiers at the base joined me in adding our names to a petition for peace published as an advertisement in the *New York Times* and signed by 1,365 service members. The ad urged people to attend the planned mobilization rally in Washington, DC on November 15, 1969. It was a time of renewed momentum for the antiwar movement following the success of the Vietnam Moratorium the month before. Several of us from the base drove down to the rally in DC and joined a contingent of several hundred soldiers amidst a crowd of nearly half a million people. Such a massive outcry for peace surely would have an impact, we felt.

As we returned to New York that evening, it seemed that every car on the New Jersey Turnpike was filled with protesters from the demonstration. The crowded rest stops along the road seemed like miniature versions of the rally. It was an empowering, joyful experience. When we returned to our car and heard the radio news, though, our spirits sank. There was Nixon's voice telling the press he paid no attention to the rally and would not be influenced by protesters. We were crushed to think that our efforts might have been for naught.

Only years later did we learn that the Moratorium events and the Washington mobilization influenced US policy and helped to prevent a major escalation of the war, as I explain in Section 4. The White House had issued an ultimatum to Hanoi threatening a massive increase in bombing if it did not end the war on American terms. Nixon wrote in his memoir that the protests and the fear of even greater opposition had dissuaded him from carrying out the planned attacks. The pressure of antiwar action limited US options and acted as a constraint on military escalation. We had more power than we knew.

1.1 Overview

I offer these stories as examples of the difficulty that activists have in recognizing success. Too often we feel powerless or believe our protests and political actions have no value. As Bill Moyer and his colleagues observed in developing the Movement Actin Plan (2001), irrational feelings of powerlessness can lead to burn-out and self-fulfilling failure (p. 5). My purpose in this work is to examine how peace movements have been effective at times in helping to end war and reduce nuclear weapons. I document instances of activist influence on policy and explore the factors that account for this impact. The focus is on questions of agency, to understand the requirements of effective social mobilization and identify strategies and methods that contribute to constructive policy change.

calculations of political parties and elected leaders (Tarrow, 1998, pp. 4, 89). The boundaries between noninstitutional and institutional forms of action are often porous.

It is important to determine what counts as peace movement activity and what does not. Activities initiated by and with antiwar and disarmament organizations can be considered part of the overall peace movement. Those that have no connection, even though they advance activist goals, would not qualify as part of the movement.

Consider the Nobel-prize-winning Pugwash Conference on Science and World Affairs, informally known as the Pugwash movement. The organization seeks a world without weapons of mass destruction and sponsors annual conferences of scientists to address nuclear security issues, but it is not part of the peace movement.

Another example would be the many statements against the Iraq War that were issued by former government officials, scientists and political scholars, including the "Don't Attack Saddam" article by former National Security Adviser Brent Scowcroft in 2002 in the *Wall Street Journal*. These and other establishment critiques gave impetus to antiwar opposition but were not part of the movement.

Campaigns are components of a movement but are distinct. They are focused, timebound activities to achieve specific policy objectives. They often emerge from social movement organizations and include coalitions with groups and individuals that are outside the peace movement. Examples would be American Against Escalation in Iraq, which won support for a timetable to withdraw US troops, and the Stop MX campaign during the freeze movement. By their nature campaigns engage political institutions. They seek to change policy by applying focused pressure on decision-makers and helping to elect pro-peace candidates.

Campaigns are sometimes confused with movements, and the reverse is also true. The titles of organizations can add to the confusion. The primary mass organization of the freeze movement from 1981 through 1986 was named the Nuclear Weapons Freeze Campaign. It was not a campaign as such, but a large-scale decentralized and locally controlled clearing house that encompassed the vast grassroots freeze movement, although it had some elements of a campaign.

Social movements employ distinct strategies and tactics. Gene Sharp differentiated between grand strategy, which is the overall goal and vision of a movement, and campaign strategies, which are specific political objectives realizable within a foreseeable time period. In support of these strategic goals movements employ an array of tactics and methods. Differences over strategy and methods can create tensions within movements as well as between movements and governments.

For the peace movement, the grand strategy is ending war and eliminating nuclear weapons. Campaign objectives have included withdrawing troops, ending nuclear testing and defunding continued war. Activists sometimes confuse these elements, focusing on tactics as if they were a strategy. They also mistake long-term strategic goals with campaign objectives. Those who demand nuclear abolition, for example, are sometimes skeptical of campaigns that have more limited objectives such as halting new weapons building. Both are worthy goals, and they fit together as a coherent policy toward disarmament. The question is which should be the primary campaign objective. Strategic analysis would suggest focusing on the latter, while continuing to make the case for the elimination of nuclear weapons.

1.3 Why Movements Matter

The ways in which social movements influence policy are not always evident. Results often emerge in unexpected ways or have effects far into the future. "It is always too early to calculate effect," writer Rebecca Solnit (2005) observed. We can never know how our actions today may influence events tomorrow. When we apply pressure, we can't predict how political establishments will respond. Movements may win even as they appear to lose.

The antiwar movement was unable to stop the invasion of Iraq, despite millions of people demonstrating in hundreds of cities around the world on February 15, 2003, the largest single day of antiwar protest in history. George W. Bush ignored the global outcry, saying he would not be influenced by "a focus group," and pushed ahead with the ill-fated invasion.

The protests and widespread public opposition to the war had multiple political impacts, however, as I identify in Section 2. Germany, Canada, Turkey and other countries refused to participate in Bush's so-called coalition of the willing. Member states of the UN Security Council refused to authorize the use of force, as their citizens marched in mass protests against war.

Opposition to the continuing war and occupation became an electoral issue in the US, helping Democrats gain control of both houses of Congress in 2006. Activists helped to elect antiwar candidates and convinced Congress to adopt a mandate for the withdrawal of troops, although Republicans rebuffed the effort. Barack Obama campaigned as an antiwar candidate with strong activist support and won the Democratic nomination and the presidency on a pledge to end the war. Once in office he wavered on the issue but eventually followed through on withdrawing the troops. More than the other two movements we examine, the Iraq case featured substantial engagement in institutional politics. Activists and legislators working in tandem exerted significant pressure for the withdrawal of troops.

The freeze movement was the largest nuclear disarmament mobilization in US history. In June 1982 a million people marched to New York's Central Park and approximately 90,000 gathered at the Rose Bowl in California to call for freezing and reversing the arms race. More than 11 million Americans voted in favor of nuclear freeze referenda that year. The US Catholic bishops and many other religious bodies issued influential public appeals for nuclear arms reduction. In Europe, millions of people marched in waves of protest to halt the deployment of US and Soviet intermediate-range missiles on the continent.

The White House rejected the freeze proposal, and NATO leaders dismissed the opposition to new missiles in Europe, but the protests influenced the political climate and had significant impacts, which I examine in Section 3. The success of the disarmament movement derived from its unprecedented mass support. Political leaders could not ignore so broad a public outcry for change.

Ronald Reagan responded to the popularity of the freeze by toning down his bellicose rhetoric and promising to negotiate for peace with the Soviets. He followed through on those pledges when Mikhail Gorbachev came to power and the two leaders agreed on unprecedented nuclear weapons reductions, including a treaty eliminating all intermediate-range missiles in Europe.

The struggle against the Vietnam war was the largest sustained antiwar movement in US history. The movement included widespread resistance to the draft and unprecedented levels of antiwar dissent and disobedience within the ranks of the military. Dozens of major rallies and assemblies occurred from 1965 to 1975. The high point of the movement was the Vietnam Moratorium in October 1969 when an estimated two million people participated in local actions against the war. President Richard Nixon declared that "under no circumstances will I be affected whatever" by the antiwar protests, but as analyzed in Section 4, the antiwar movement imposed significant constraints on the conduct of the war and led to the eventual withdrawal of US troops.

Continuous mass protests generated unrelenting pressure for peace. Resistance to the draft and defiance within the military reduced military capabilities and impeded the war effort. The electoral challenge to Lyndon Johnson ended troop escalation, and legislative efforts eventually cut off funding for continued war. It was the combination of all these forms of opposition, noninstitutional and institutional, that finally brought the slaughter to an end.

These observations are not meant to suggest that peace movements were the only force shaping public opinion and changing policy in these settings. Political decisions on major matters of state usually have multiple causes. During the Iraq and Vietnam wars, attitudes were shaped by the lack of military success and rising US casualty levels. During the freeze era a sea change in public opinion occurred with the realization that few could survive a nuclear war (Yankelovich & Doble, 1984).

Other causal factors could be identified in each case, all of them flowing together and combining with peace activism to exert influence on political decision-making. The constant pressure of protest and citizen action was decisive, however, bursting forth often in major rallies and events, shaping the terms of debate and raising the political and social costs of continuing objectionable policies.

Research by Jeffrey Knopf (1998) confirmed that protest movements have been a significant factor in shifting government preferences toward international cooperation. His study of four cases of arms control dialogue with the Soviet Union found that US decisions to engage in negotiations were shaped by activist pressure. Quantitative analysis showed that the level of social protest was a statistically significant variable in predicting successful talks, while none of the control variables, such as the balance of military forces and prior improvement in US-Soviet relations, were significant. As Knopf concluded "peace movements can make a difference" (p. 247).

Change often comes slowly and in unrecognized ways, amidst ambiguity and competing claims for credit. Policy adjustments rarely come quickly enough for activists or in the manner they intend. Those who campaign against war and nuclear weapons are rarely satisfied with modest victories such as gradual troop withdrawals or limits on specific weapons. Yet partial steps can be significant and may lead to more substantive change. The Iraq, nuclear freeze and Vietnam antiwar movements had political impacts that deserve to be acknowledged, and that can provide guidance for addressing the challenges of today.

1.4 Protest and Politics

Some activists and scholars see a sharp distinction between movements and institutional politics. They believe the role of movements is to criticize politicians from the outside, not to support candidates for office or lobby for legislation on the inside. Studies of nonviolent action and civil resistance examine mobilization strategies and methods but disregard activist involvement in lobbying or electoral activity (Chenoweth, 2021; Sharp, 2005). In their important work on the Iraq antiwar movement, Michael Heaney and Fabio Rojas (2023) acknowledge activist involvement in the 2006 congressional elections and the Obama campaign but describe it as the "collapse" of the movement. They assered that the election of Obama "spelled doom for the antiwar movement" (p. 229).

These assessments are too narrow, I believe. They fail to acknowledge that movements often seek to influence policy through institutional politics. Activists played a significant role in turning Congress against the Iraq War and helped to elect a president who campaigned on a promise to end the conflict. Demonstrations and protests became less frequent after the invasion, but the antiwar movement remained active and utilized both inside and outside methods to press for an end to the occupation.

The debate over street protest and institutional politics also existed in the nuclear freeze movement of the 1980s. The original strategy of the Freeze Campaign was to build a base of support in states and local congressional districts before engaging in national political campaigns. This reflected the essential grassroots nature of the movement. Its theory of change was that the political power necessary to halt the arms race would not come from the political establishment in Washington but would have to flow from the bottom up. Attempting to enter national politics prematurely would do more harm than good, the Freeze Campaign strategy argued (Solo, 1988). When members of Congress began to endorse the freeze and introduced legislation on its behalf, however, the movement could not ignore the process and allow politicians to speak for their issue. The Freeze Campaign became involved in the debate and organized grassroots participation in support of the legislation.

The Vietnam antiwar movement focused predominantly on organizing street protests rather than campaigning in elections or lobbying Congress. Some sectarian groups were opposed to institutional politics on principle and seemed more interested in overthrowing the state than working within it for policy change. As the costs of the war mounted and opposition grew, opportunities for institutional engagement began to emerge, although activists faced obstacles and opposition from hardliners in both parties. In 1968 liberal Democrats effectively challenged President Lyndon Johnson in the Democratic primaries, but party bosses gave the nomination to Johnson loyalist Hubert Humphrey, who lost to Richard Nixon. Antiwar stalwart George McGovern won the Democratic Party nomination in 1972 but was trounced by Nixon.

Legislative efforts to end the war achieved major success in 1973 when Congress used its power of the purse to prohibit any further US bombing or military operations in Southeast Asia. Activists subsequently applied pressure on Congress to cut military funding for the South Vietnamese and Cambodian governments, which finally brought the fighting to a close.

Those who dismiss activist involvement in conventional politics have a truncated view of social movements. As Tom Hayden (2007) observed in his analysis of opposition to the Iraq War, the peace movement cannot be defined solely on the basis of action in the streets. Movements are forms of social contestation that sometimes overlap with electoral or legislative activity (Tarrow, 2012). Movements "straddle the boundaries between institutional and the extra-institutional politics," wrote David Meyer and Catherine Corrigall-Brown (2005, p. 329). Most activists are pragmatic about their choice of methods, demonstrating in the streets but also engaging in electoral organizing and legislative lobbying. Sharp boundaries between street protest and conventional politics are rare.

Knopf found that activist engagement with political institutions was strongly associated with success in gaining policy shifts in favor of arms control. He identified three mechanisms through which activists were able to shape policy preferences: (1) mobilizing public participation in elections, (2) engaging with sympathetic legislators to alter issue priorities and realign congressional coalitions and (3) generating new ideas and proposals for adoption by government actors. Each mechanism involved interaction with the decision-making process (Knopf, 1998, pp. 73–78).

1.5 How Do Movements Succeed?

To assess how protest leads to policy change, we need to address two prior questions. How do we define success, and how do movements bring about change?

Success is usually defined as the fulfillment of movement demands and goals. But which goals? If we consider the grand strategy and long-term vision of the peace movement – ending war and eliminating nuclear weapons – success clearly is a long way off. If we look more concretely at campaign objectives and policy goals, however, the picture brightens. We see evidence of many successes for the peace movement globally and in the US, although the gains are often piecemeal and fall short of campaign demands. Activists are rarely satisfied with incremental gains and may not recognize them as a result of their action.

There is also the law of unintended effect. Movements can never know exactly how political leaders will respond to the pressures they apply. Decision-makers claim to ignore movement demands, but they are often forced to respond, although not in the way activists anticipate. The result may be policy twists that are unfamiliar and are not easily traceable to movement pressures.

We know that peace movements have been successful at times in shaping policy, but how do they exert that influence? One approach, the most prevalent and the primary focus of social movement analysis, is the mobilization of social action to protest grievances and place issues and demands on the public agenda. The second approach is activist engagement in legislative lobbying and electoral activity, which can exert direct influence on policymaking. The two approaches correspond to noninstitutional and institutional politics, outside action and inside engagement. As emphasized throughout this study, the two approaches often work in tandem to bring about policy change.

The ability of a movement to shape public consciousness and generate support for policy demands depends on many factors. One of the most important is the scale of public participation. To be credible and effective, movements need to have a large public following. Scholars of civil resistance identify mass participation as decisive to campaign effectiveness. Erica Chenoweth (2021) argues that "the single most important influence on a civil resistance campaign's success is the scale and range of popular participation" (pp. 3–4, 83).

Large-scale public protests are an important means of demonstrating mass support. They attract media attention and give visibility and voice to underrepresented constituencies. If they have sufficient scale and are part of a persistent pattern of public action, they can change the calculations of decision-makers and shape the political climate in ways that are conducive to movement goals.

Mass participation is also manifest at local levels through grassroots mobilization. Movements exert influence not only through singular mass rallies but in multiple actions locally. In each of the movements under review large protests in major cities were accompanied by smaller actions in dozens and sometimes hundreds of local communities.

Local nuclear freeze groups sprang up in nearly every major city and many smaller communities. They organized public forums, religious services and educational events at the grassroot level. Many also engaged in institutional politics: participating in nationally coordinated legislative lobbying, organizing delegation visits with their congressional representatives in Washington and in the home district, and holding vigils or protests outside their local offices.

The Vietnam movement was active in cities and local communities all over the country. Student protests occurred at many universities, not just at elite schools but also at many state and community schools (Kershner, 2023). Protest and resistance actions occurred at hundreds of local draft boards, and actions in support of antiwar soldiers occurred outside dozens of military bases (Carver et al., 2019; Foley, 2003).

All these and more are forms of citizen participation. When considered across a whole movement they amount to many groups, with many thousands of local participants at peak moments of engagement. This form of activity is harder to quantify than crowd-counting estimates, but it is a major part of the political influence of the peace movement in specific campaigns and overall.

Effective campaigning requires the ability to combine visionary goals with practical and achievable objectives. The visionary goal is necessary to motivate activists, but concrete practical objectives are necessary to attract a mass following. They are also helpful for building the coalitions that are vital for effective campaigns. Achievable campaign objectives can help to attract those who are not already part of the movement and who may not share the broader vision. For the peace movement this means identifying near-term objectives, such as preventing a new arms race, while also expressing support for a world without nuclear weapons.

Movements emerge in response to political grievances. Public discontent can establish the basis for mobilization, but to organize campaigns that address grievances, it is necessary to articulate constructive alternatives. This helps to establish movement credibility and is essential for engaging in institutional politics.

Communications and effective message framing are essential for movement effectiveness. Every political contest is at its core a struggle over the meaning of words and ideas and the framing of news and information. As William Gamson observed, the images and metaphors activists convey are central to their prospects for political success. (Gamson, 1990). Messages are more likely to be internalized and acted upon if they resonate with widely shared values and beliefs such as fairness and safety.

For the peace movement, which contests military policy, patriotism is one of those core values. It helps activists avoid being portrayed as anti-military or disrespectful of those who serve. A model for patriotic messaging was the billboard displayed in 2003 by the group Working Assets, featuring a "Support our Troops" banner along with a yellow ribbon with the bolded message: "Bring Them Home Now." (Cortright, 2023, p. 77).

Mass mobilization and public communications campaigns often coexist with legislative lobbying and electoral activity. Institutional approaches involve direct contact with decision-makers and voters rather than performative action for mass audiences. Political engagement is the arena where movement demands are translated directly into policy.

1.6 Movement Dynamics

Movements inevitably experience waves of ebb and flow. They grow to massive scale in response to particularly outrageous events or policies – such as the invasion of Iraq, and an escalating threat of nuclear war – and they ebb or flow in relation to events that affect that policy. Eventually all movements go through periods of decline and fade away. The process of forming and disbanding groups is an inherent part of movement organizing. Movements often change shape as new challenges arise, and they tend to shift toward institutional forms of action as opportunities for political engagement materialize.

The degree to which activists emphasize street protest or conventional politics depends on multiple variables. Social movement scholars emphasize the importance of political opportunity structures, which can be defined as the presence or absence of avenues for engaging politically (Tilly & Tarrow, 2015). One of those opportunities is access to the established political system. If there are viable legislative options for ending or constraining war, or if there are electable candidates who are committed to working for peace and disarmament, activists will be encouraged by these opportunities and will devote more of their time, energy, and money to working within the system and engaging in conventional forms of political action (McAdam & Tarrow, 2010).

Perceptions of success affect these choices. As public discontent deepens and elected officials became more openly critical, activists see the political odds shifting in their favor. They become more involved in lobbying and electoral work rather than marching and protesting. Often both forms of action occur during the same period. Many activists participate in street action and institutional politics and move seamlessly back and forth between the two.

A sequential pattern is visible in all three movements. In the early stages of the movements, when legislative or electoral approaches were closed or unsuccessful, protest action became the primary venue for raising political demands. Activists mobilized in the streets and worked for peace from the outside. Over time, as protest action helped to generate pressure, opportunities appeared for conventional political action. Activists changed their role from outside rebels to change agents seeking reform within the system (Moyer et al., 2001, pp. 21–41).

The next three sections provide summary reviews of the Iraq antiwar, nuclear freeze and Vietnam antiwar movements. I examine how each influenced public opinion and shaped the political climate and trace their policy impacts. I review strategies and methods in each movement separately and collectively and evaluate how they affected policy outcomes. From these reflections I offer a set of general observations for effective social mobilization as a guide for future peace and disarmament movements. In the final section I draw from the experience of the freeze movement to explore options for seeking a halt to the development of new nuclear bombs and enhanced weapons systems today.

2 Opposing the Invasion and Occupation of Iraq

In the struggle to prevent an unprovoked war of aggression against Iraq, the battle to influence public opinion was paramount. Polls showed that a majority of Americans favored the use of force to remove Saddam Hussein from power. Traumatized by the horrors of the 9/11 attacks, Americans were fearful and angry and were susceptible to manipulation and demands for revenge. The Bush administration took advantage of the public trauma to amplify fear and hatred of Saddam Hussein, linking him falsely to Al Qaeda and the violent extremists who attacked the US. The White House rejected the "unequivocal conclusion" of the intelligence community that Iraq had nothing to do with 9/11 (Riedel, 2021).

The administration flooded the airwaves with messages claiming that the Iraqi dictator possessed and would use weapons of mass destruction (WMD).

In response, the antiwar movement challenged the evidence for such claims and argued for alternatives to war. Activists warned that military intervention would cause the deaths of many innocent civilians and lead to more terrorism, not less. The movement's message, delivered at protest actions and in media events, was to give UN inspectors more time to search for WMDs. Antiwar messaging also emphasized the lack of UN authorization for the use of force.

The constant questioning of the justification for war began to have an impact on public opinion. A Gallup poll for CNN and USA Today found approval of an invasion declining from 74 percent in November 2001 to 53 percent in August 2002 (Mazarr, 2019, p. 224; Moore, 2002). President Bush was frustrated by the lack of international support and worried about the erosion of public opinion. In January 2003 he confided to National Security Adviser Condoleezza Rice, "we are not winning" in the debate to oust Hussein. "Time is not on our side here." On the eve of the invasion he told the prime ministers of Spain and Portugal that it was necessary to launch the invasion immediately because "public opinion won't get better, and it will get worse in some countries like America" (Woodward, 2004, pp. 253–254, 357).

2.1 The World Says No

Bush had reason to be worried amidst a massive global mobilization against war. Protests against attacking Iraq began in 2002 and continued in a crescendo of mass action to the historic worldwide demonstrations of February 15, 2003, the largest single day of antiwar protest in history. An estimated ten million people participated in demonstrations in hundreds of cities in dozens of countries on every continent. More than a million people gathered in London, an estimated two million rallied in Rome, and hundreds of thousands demonstrated in Madrid, Barcelona, Berlin, Tokyo, Sydney, Cairo, New York and other cities (Cortright, 2023, pp. 1, 48–53).

The global antiwar rallies provided dramatic evidence of the public opposition that worried Bush and British Prime Minister Tony Blair. Despite their constant efforts at public persuasion, the two leaders were unable to win the argument for war. A Gallup poll in late February 2003 showed support for military action drifting downward again after a brief bump in approval following Secretary of State Colin Powell's presentation of the case for war at the UN earlier that month. Surveys showed majorities in favor of giving UN inspectors more time and opposed to an invasion without UN approval (Cramer, 2007, p. 521; Kull et al., 2003/2004, p. 569). In the UK, Blair managed to win parliamentary approval, but he was never able to gain a public majority for waging war without UN approval (Strong, 2017).

The February 2003 rallies were not the only protests against the invasion and occupation of Iraq. From 2002 through 2007 there were eight antiwar demonstrations in the United States that attracted estimated crowds of 100,000 or more participants each, ranking the Iraq peace movement as among the largest in US history (Hayden, 2007, p. 126). Noam Chomsky observed that protests against the Iraq War were "at a far higher level than they were with regard to Vietnam at comparable stages of the invasions" (Knickerbocker, 2007).

Although the enormous outpouring of antiwar protests did not stop the invasion, it illustrated the importance of mass participation in giving legitimacy to the antiwar movement. The huge demonstrations and global scale of the opposition enhanced the credibility of antiwar voices and established the critical mass that is necessary to exert policy influence. The episode also revealed that while mass participation is necessary for movement credibility, it is not always sufficient to guarantee political success, especially when faced with obdurate, un-listening leaders like Bush and Blair.

2.2 Congressional Failure

A major blow to the cause of peace came in October 2002 when the US Congress voted to approve the use of force in Iraq. Once that vote occurred, peace advocates lost a major institutional pathway for trying to block the invasion. The failure was not that of the movement but of Senators and Representatives who naively swallowed administration deceptions, thinking the vote was to bolster diplomacy rather than to wage war. As the debate began Senate leaders tried to place limits on the use of force. Senator Carl Levin, chair of the Senate Armed Services Committee, offered a resolution requiring prior authorization by the UN Security Council. The White House brushed aside all attempts to restrict the scope of military action and won overwhelming approval for a blank check resolution authorizing Bush to use force "as he determines."

All of this took place before the major antiwar coalitions, the United for Peace and Justice, and Win Without War, were created. Some peace groups attempted to persuade members of Congress to vote against the use of force, but their efforts were too little too late. The vote was pushed through rapidly with little time for public debate or participation.

The irony is that a previously announced antiwar demonstration took place in Washington on October 26, two weeks after the fateful congressional vote. That protest was organized by ANSWER, Act Now to Stop War and End Racism, a radical splinter group ideologically opposed to institutional politics that organizes street protests. The demonstration and others that followed were large, but their impact might have been greater if they had focused on pressuring members of Congress in Washington and in their local districts.

2.3 Policy Impacts

When the massive global protests failed to prevent the invasion, many activists were depressed. Some considered the movement a failure. The evidence indicates, however, that public opposition had significant indirect effects, which weakened the US war effort and contributed to the US strategic defeat in Iraq.

As part of its argument for military action, the White House espoused the fiction that the invasion would be a short, simple operation welcomed by the Iraqi people. Senior military commanders knew better and told administration officials that at least 450,000 troops would be needed to conquer and police Iraq. Secretary of Defense Donald Rumsfeld (2012) dismissed the advice of his generals and cut the invasion force to one-third that size (p. 438). The decision to deny military needs was a product of hubris, but it also served the political purpose of quelling concerns about the likely costs of the operation. To admit otherwise and acknowledge the required sacrifices would have empowered antiwar critics and made the war harder to sell politically.

The same considerations prompted the administration's decisions to defer postwar planning and downplay preparations for the occupation. Many analysts argued that postwar planning for Iraq was atrociously flawed and incomplete. "In fact, it was unconscionable," wrote Brookings Institution analyst Michael O'Hanlon (2005). The reason for the deceit, he wrote, was to promote the illusion of a quick and easy war "in order to assure domestic and international support."

These political decisions, considered necessary to quell public doubts, ultimately doomed the mission. This is the conclusion of the US Army War College history of the Iraq War (Godfroy et al., 2019). The US failed to attain its strategic objectives in Iraq, the study concluded. The authors identified many reasons for this failure but emphasized one factor above all, the lack of sufficient troops. They wrote: "Strategic defeat was almost assured by artificial constraints" and the "overall shortage of ground forces;" commanders had "too few troops to accomplish their military missions." The report took direct aim at what it called a "short-war assumption," noting that US leaders "deluded themselves" about the commitment required. The analysis traced the administration's strategic errors to "domestic political considerations" (Godfroy et al., 2019, pp. 619, 622, 627).

Political opposition to the war was the most important of those domestic considerations and had significant unintended effects. It prompted the Bush administration to make policy decisions that led to strategic failure. To maintain the claim of a short military operation, the administration went to war with insufficient force and without proper planning. To do otherwise, to plan for an occupation and send the number of troops requested by military commanders, would have been to admit that a major war was in the offing. This would have fueled the growing public opposition.

The troop shortage issue and the challenges of battling the insurgency imposed significant hardships on service members in the all-volunteer force. The mission in Iraq and the parallel war in Afghanistan forced many soldiers to serve multiple combat tours. For the first time in modern history, large numbers of National Guard and Reserve soldiers were activated and deployed for combat. Service members approaching the end of their contracts were involuntarily extended – "stop loss" it was called. Many service members and military family members complained, and some organized actions against the war. Nearly 3,000 current service members signed an Appeal for Redress urging withdrawal from Iraq. Their action was featured on CBS' *60 Minutes* in February 2007 (Hutto, 2008). Dozens of other protests against the war and the conditions of service occurred among soldiers and military family members. Morale problems and dissent were not supposed to happen among those who volunteer for service, but men and women who join the military do not sign away their consciences. They will object when deployed for dubious purposes.

The public skepticism fanned by the antiwar movement deepened after the invasion when US forces found no WMDs in Iraq and a fierce insurgency ensued. The war became a costly military fiasco, wrote Tom Ricks (2006). As the fighting dragged on, opposition to the military mission mounted and demands for withdrawing US troops gained political traction. The arguments of the movement were proven correct.

Through multiple threads of influence, the antiwar mobilization helped to shape public consciousness and had far-reaching policy consequences. The phrase "ending endless war" entered public consciousness. It began as a movement bumper sticker but over time became a slogan of political candidates and a basis for policy. Reluctance to put boots on the ground in foreign conflicts became a hallmark of national security policy.

The skepticism about military intervention coursing through American politics in recent years comes from many sources. Probably the greatest factor is public revulsion at the disastrous record of US military interventions, which have led to catastrophic failures, exorbitant costs, incalculable loss of life and the spread of violence and instability in the Middle East and beyond (Gordan, 2020). An opinion poll in 2019 found 62 percent of Americans agreeing that invading Iraq was a mistake (p. 261). The doubts initially sown by peace advocates became the majority opinion.

2.4 Global Implications

International opposition to the Iraq War also contributed to the US strategic failure. The UN Security Council's refusal to authorize the use of force was unprecedented. It was the first time since the United Nations was founded, wrote Immanuel Wallerstein, "that the United States, on an issue that mattered [strategically], could not get a majority on the Security Council" (2003, p. 28). The Council's reluctance was the result of the widespread global opposition to the war.

The interplay between the antiwar movement and the United Nations was pivotal. Member states of the UN were opposed to the war but were powerless to stop it. The UN Security Council by its design is captive to the permanent powers, and when its most powerful member is bent on aggression, the UN has no capacity to prevent it. The power of the Security Council lies in its authority to confer international legitimacy. When it withholds consent, as it did twice in rejecting US requests for authority to use force, it denies legitimacy. It was able to do so because of the worldwide antiwar movement.

A creative dialectic developed between the Security Council and the transnational peace movement. The public opposition to war hinged on the lack of UN authorization. Objections at the UN in turn depended on the strength of public opinion. In Germany, Turkey and other countries, polls showed 80 percent or more of respondents opposing military action (Pew, 2003). Massive protests against the war occurred in the capitals of Security Council member states and in many other countries. The stronger the global opposition to the war, the greater the determination of UN diplomats to resist US pressure. The stronger the objections at the UN, the greater the legitimacy and impact of the antiwar movement. It was a unique form of global political synergy. By defending the UN, despite its many shortcomings, the movement prevented the internationalization of the war and weakened the military effort.

Bush's so-called coalition of the willing was a threadbare arrangement that provided little help for the US mission. The massive scale of public opposition prevented many countries from joining the coalition and convinced most of those that did participate to limit their role to noncombat duties. Spain initially sent troops, but they were withdrawn a year later when national elections brought socialists to power on an antiwar platform. The US Army War College study of the war says the coalition was "largely unsuccessful" at the operational level (Godfroy et al., 2019, p. 616). American troops did almost all of the fighting in the war and suffered 93 percent of the casualties.

The legacy of the antiwar movement continued after the conflict was over. When military strikes against Syria were proposed in August 2013, as a response to the Assad regime's use of chemical weapons, opposition quickly developed.

The House of Commons in Britain denied the request to use force by a 295–272 vote, the first parliamentary rejection of a request to use force since 1782 (Strong, 2017, pp. 2, 176.) Opposition to military action also emerged in the US. With congressional and public skepticism mounting, the Obama administration opted to refrain from military action. The shadow of Iraq loomed large over these debates (Singer, 2013).

2.5 To the Ballot Box

Although activists in the US were unsuccessful at preventing the invasion, opposition to the war and occupation continued. Some activists turned to the use of electoral and legislative levers of power as a means of generating pressure to bring the troops home. This was an example of inside and outside approaches combining to build pressure for ending the war. Although the results of the movement's political engagement were uneven and ultimately fell short of what activists wanted, the cumulative impacts were significant.

The antiwar movement's first foray into electoral politics came in June 2003 when former Vermont Governor Howard Dean raised a stir during a meeting of the Democratic National Committee by asking party officials why they had not opposed the invasion of Iraq. Dean had no organizational connection to the antiwar movement, but he understood the political salience of the Iraq issue and urged Democrats to take advantage of it. His question was an uncomfortable one for party leaders who had voted for the October 2002 congressional resolution authorizing the use of force in Iraq.

Until that time Dean's plan to enter the Democratic Party primaries in 2004 seemed a quixotic and forlorn quest. As soon as he raised the Iraq question, his campaign came alive and was flooded with volunteers, many of them from the peace movement. Dean suddenly rose to number one in presidential opinion polls, although he did poorly in the Iowa caucus and New Hampshire primary, and his campaign quickly faded.

The force driving this sudden surge of support for Dean and interest in the 2004 election was MoveOn, which has been closely aligned with the Democratic Party. The network grew into an internet powerhouse through its opposition to the war and support for Win Without War. MoveOn activists pointed to the Dean campaign as an early indication of the potential impact of the antiwar issue for mobilizing support within the Democratic Party.

In the 2004 presidential campaign Senator John Kerry was unable to harness that activist energy. His 2002 Senate vote to authorize the use of force in Iraq haunted him at every turn. He was critical of Bush's handling of the war but did not campaign as an antiwar candidate or advocate the withdrawal of troops as activists wanted. As late as August 2004, Kerry said that he stood by his vote on the war. His stance on the war was like an albatross that dragged down and ultimately doomed his candidacy.

2.6 Turning Congress

For MoveOn, the shock of Bush's reelection was a wake-up call. The organization doubled down on its strategy of harnessing antiwar sentiment at the ballot box. Polling results showed that the Iraq issue had the strongest influence in motivating a political commitment from MoveOn supporters and, more importantly, from likely voters. The result was an "intense flow of antiwar energy during the 2006 electoral season," as the congressional elections became an antiwar battleground (Hayden, 2007, pp. 147–148, 158–159).

The opening skirmish in the 2006 campaign came in Connecticut when local activists mounted a challenge to pro-war Senator Joe Lieberman in the Democratic primary. MoveOn and other groups threw their support behind antiwar critic and Connecticut business executive Ned Lamont who challenged Lieberman on the war issue. Lamont scored an upset victory in the early August primary vote. As the *New York Times* reported, Lamont "soared from nowhere on a fierce antiwar message [and] won a narrow but decisive victory" (Healy, 2006). The outcome in Connecticut sent shockwaves through Washington and showed Democratic candidates across the country the power of the antiwar message in motivating voters. Although Lieberman held on to his seat in the November election by running as an Independent and winning Republican support, the lesson of the Lamont campaign was clear. Democratic candidates could win on an antiwar message.

Peace activists were heavily involved in many local races that year and played a significant role in the election of dozens of candidates who were committed to withdrawing troops from Iraq. MoveOn launched a nationwide independent expenditure campaign that targeted fifty-five House campaigns and twelve Senate races, focusing on vulnerable Republicans in suburban districts. Campaign activities included hiring dozens of local organizers to work in targeted districts to mobilize thousands of campaign volunteers for voter education and turnout. Many of those volunteers were antiwar activists. They were shifting from protest to policy and returning to their primary identity as Democrats (Heaney & Rojas, 2015).

The November 2006 vote was a decisive victory for the Democratic Party and a turning point in the politics of the war. Democrats picked up thirty-one seats in the House and six in the Senate. In Virginia, combat veteran and former Secretary of the Navy Jim Webb pulled off an upset victory based on his opposition to the war against heavily favored incumbent Senator George Allen (Moser, B., 2006).

In Minnesota, political newcomer Tim Walz won a dramatic upset victory in the rural 1st Congressional District running on an antiwar platform.

Republicans failed to win any seats held by Democrats in either the Senate or the House (Holsti, 2011, p. 145). For the first time in twelve years, the Democrats controlled both houses of Congress, a result widely seen as swayed by antiwar sentiment. Other issues also influenced the vote that fall, but the dominant concern was Iraq. Gallup polls prior to the election showed the war in Iraq as the most important issue for likely voters, selected as the top government priority by 61 percent of Democrats and 52 percent of Independents. Editorial page punditry and exit-poll surveys agreed: Iraq was the "Archimedean lever" that shifted independent voters massively toward the Democrats (Davis, 2007). The results of the 2006 election sent a clear message that antiwar activists were a force to be reckoned with in the Democratic Party – a message not lost on the junior senator from Illinois.

2.7 The Antiwar Lobby

The Democratic victory in 2006 dramatically improved the prospects for legislative action to end the war. Antiwar lobbying efforts had begun a couple of years before, as an Out-of-Iraq caucus emerged within the House of Representatives (Heaney & Rojas, 2015, p. 175). Initial legislative efforts were unsuccessful in the Republican-controlled Congress, but the situation changed in 2007. MoveOn, Win Without War, United for Peace and Justice and other groups mounted a major lobbying effort to win congressional support for establishing a timetable for the withdrawal of troops. Bush ignored demands for withdrawal and doubled down on the war by ordering a "surge" of additional troops to Iraq. Activists were infuriated, as were many Democratic Party officials. The House voted 246–182 for a nonbinding resolution opposing the surge (Baker, 2014, p. 542). A majority in the Senate also disapproved, but Bush pushed ahead.

In response to Bush's policy, MoveOn brought together the Service Employees International Union, Win Without War, US Action and other organizations in a new coalition, Americans Against Escalation in Iraq (AAEI). The purpose of the new grouping was to mobilize political opposition to the war through a focused legislative campaign for the withdrawal of troops. Its aim was to build opposition to the war in local districts. The campaign organized hundreds of local events and meetings with legislators, integrating the mobilization of grassroots activism in local districts with lobbying efforts on Capitol Hill. The legislative campaign was a model of inside and outside action to achieve political results. The lobbying efforts were fueled by persistent grassroot mobilization in key local districts, as activists pressured their Senators and Representative to vote for specific legislation to withdraw troops.

The lobbying campaign involved uncomfortable compromises. Peace groups demanded an end to the occupation and immediate withdrawal of troops. To gain the support of members of Congress, however, AAEI organizers had to settle for legislative language proposing a timetable for withdrawal rather than an immediate exit. They also had to accept substituting the word redeployment for withdrawal. This change came from Congress members who were fearful of being branded weak on defense or lacking in support for the troops. Redeployment meant the same thing in terms of requiring the removal of troops from Iraq, but it implied a willingness to accept the presence of troops elsewhere.

Activists were decidedly cool to the redeployment stratagem. They opposed military intervention in all countries. They went along with using the term, though, recognizing that the specific language of the resolution was less important than the act of putting Congress on record in favor of removing US troops from Iraq. It was a classic case of accepting compromise in service of a larger strategic goal, which is often part of the process of attempting to translate protest into policy.

A similar debate occurred during the nuclear freeze movement when the congressional nuclear freeze resolution of May 2003 became weighted down with compromise and qualifications. Activists supported the measure nonetheless as a symbolic statement implying that the House of Representatives was voting in favor of the freeze.

Opponents of the Iraq War scored three legislative victories in 2007 on binding language establishing a timetable for removing troops. The first vote was in March when the House of Representatives voted 218–212 to approve the measure (Angle, 2007). The Senate followed suit, but the victory was short-lived when President Bush exercised a presidential veto in May to kill the measure. In July, the House voted again to set a timeline for withdrawal, this time by a slightly wider margin, 223–201. In the fall, congressional leaders introduced a new bill, the Orderly and Responsible Iraq Redeployment Appropriations Act, directing the president to commence an immediate removal of troops from Iraq. The House of Representatives approved the bill by a vote of 218 to 203 in November. The Senate voted in favor by a 53 to 45 margin in December, but under filibuster voting rules in force at the time, sixty votes were needed for Senate passage, and the measure failed (Elsea et al., 2008). Despite majority backing from both houses of Congress, the mandate for troop withdrawal did not become law.

The Senate and House votes were nonetheless significant in demonstrating a congressional consensus against the occupation and in favor of a timetable for withdrawal. The Bush administration began removing troops sooner and more completely than military planners wanted. The White House hoped to keep a residual American force in Iraq for an extended period, but political leaders in Baghdad refused and insisted on a timeline for complete US withdrawal. In July 2008, Bush yielded to Iraqi demands, and after further haggling the two sides signed a security agreement in November for the status of US forces that called for complete withdrawal by the end of 2011 (Baker, 2014, pp. 601, 619–620).

2.8 Electing a President

From the very beginning of the presidential race, Barack Obama won the support of many antiwar activists. The principal distinction of his candidacy was his forthright stance against the war. Obama (2020) writes in his memoir that the Iraq War was the biggest issue for his campaign (p. 158). Hillary Clinton was heavily favored going into the Democratic primaries, with substantial financial backing and the support of many Democratic Party leaders, but she waffled on ending the war and was burdened by her October 2002 Senate vote in favor of the use of force. Obama by contrast had spoken against the invasion at an antiwar rally in Chicago the week before the Senate vote, and he remained unequivocally opposed to the war, vowing to end it if elected. His campaign expressed "an unapologetic antiwar boldness," wrote journalist Spencer Ackerman (2021, p. 114).

The Obama candidacy was a political opportunity for the movement, and many activists embraced it. When MoveOn conducted an internal poll of its online members to determine which candidate the organization should support in the primaries, 70 percent of respondents endorsed Obama (Hayes, 2008). This brought with it a massive wave of volunteer and financial support from antiwar activists.

Obama's electoral strategy played to the strengths of this activist constituency. His campaign created an extensive field presence in dozens of states, built on the foundations of already existing activist networks – principally the antiwar movement, but also labor, women's, environmentalist, African American, Latino, and other established organizing networks.

Obama's victories were concentrated in caucus states, where success is determined by the strength of local activist support rather than big name endorsements and large television advertising budgets. In Texas, Clinton won the popular vote, but Obama won more of the caucuses and ended up with the majority of the state's delegates. He also benefitted from a surge of African American votes, especially in the South, following his unexpected victory in the Iowa caucus. The national popular vote was extremely close, but Obama held a significant margin in the thirteen caucus contests, enough to win the nomination. Obama's victory was the result of a superior ability to mobilize tens of thousands of strongly committed loyalists from the antiwar movement, the African American community and other activist networks (Jeralyn, 2008).

That support base also propelled Obama to victory in the general election. According to researcher David Karpf (2012), during the course of the 2008 election, MoveOn channeled almost $100 million in campaign contributions and one million volunteers to the Obama campaign (p. 29). It was one of the most influential organizations supporting the Democratic Party in the election that year. The Obama campaign pioneered the use of social media to harness volunteer and donor support, building a network of 13 million people on its various email and Facebook lists. Many of these names were drawn from the MoveOn list (which had grown to 5 million) and other pre-existing activist networks. With 8 million visitors a month, the Obama website was used to create 35,000 volunteer groups and organize 200,000 offline events. The campaign had 3 million online donors and received a total of 6.5 million contributions, with an average gift size of $80. Obama raised twice as much money as Republican candidate John McCain, a record $750 million, two-thirds of which came from small contributions (Lutz, 2009; UPI, 2008; Walker, 2008).

Many activists supported Obama because of his opposition to the war, but they had few illusions about his views on other foreign policy issues. In his 2002 speech at the antiwar rally in Chicago, he declared, "I don't oppose all wars. What I am opposed to is a dumb war" (Obama, 2020, p. 47). During his 2008 campaign, he reiterated his commitment to withdraw troops from Iraq, but he was equally clear in pledging to increase military involvement in Afghanistan. He vowed to use force wherever he deemed necessary to counter terrorist threats. As president he ordered a surge of troops to Afghanistan and launched hundreds of drone strikes in Pakistan, much to the chagrin of many antiwar activists who had supported him. Yet on the issue that mattered most, withdrawing troops and ending the occupation of Iraq, Obama fulfilled his promise to voters. The pressure and support of the antiwar movement helped to make that possible.

In July 2008, after winning the Democratic nomination, Obama visited the troops in Iraq. He was under pressure from diplomats and many in the Pentagon to agree on maintaining a sizable troop presence in Iraq. Commanding General David Petraeus hosted Obama's visit and tried to talk him out of setting a deadline for withdrawal, urging him to keep a residual force. Obama listened respectfully but disagreed with the general, as he recounts in his memoir. He refused to back off on the commitment to withdraw US forces (Obama, 2020, pp. 157–159).

After taking office, Obama delayed and hesitated on the issue as pressure for a residual force persisted, but members of the Iraqi government remained adamant in opposing further US military involvement (Kahl, 2014). In December 2011, the White House announced that the last troops had left the country. Obama's decision was made easier by the fact that he was following the timeline originally established by the Bush administration.

The results of antiwar electoral and lobbying efforts were a disappointment for many activists. The movement was successful in the 2006 elections and won major congressional votes in favor of withdrawing troops in 2007, but those measures did not become law, and the occupation continued. Opponents of the war played a role in helping Obama become president in 2008, but many were impatient with the slow pace of the withdrawal timeline and frustrated by his waffling. The antiwar movement nonetheless demonstrated significant political strength in pressuring Congress to establish limits on the US presence in Iraq and helping to elect members of Congress and a president committed to ending the war.

Activists sometimes conflate conventional politics and the role of social movements. They tend to project their own values and goals onto politicians and become disillusioned when their demands are not met in the manner they want. In the process, Hayden (2007) observed, they "run the danger of underestimating the impact they are actually achieving" (pp. 170–172). They fail to recognize incremental or limited policy changes as a sign of movement success. The Iraq antiwar movement did not accomplish all that activists wanted, but it achieved political successes that are of historic importance, and that deserve to be acknowledged by activists, and by scholars.

3 Mobilizing to Freeze and Reverse the Arms Race

The proposal for a bilateral nuclear weapons freeze that emerged from arms control researchers and peace activists in the late 1970s sparked the largest US disarmament movement in modern history. The result was an unprecedented public outcry against the threat of nuclear war that significantly influenced policy, although few recognized it at the time and political leaders publicly dismissed the movement.

The freeze was a succinct proposal for a bilateral US–Soviet halt to the development, testing and deployment of nuclear weapons. It was embodied in the Call to Halt the Arms Race, authored by MIT researcher Randall Forsberg, who became an articulate and forceful spokesperson for the issue. The appeal of the freeze was its simplicity and accessibility to the average citizen. The concept was eagerly embraced by citizens who at the time were alarmed by an accelerating arms race and the increased risk of nuclear war. The freeze directed its appeal to the Soviet Union as well as the United States, thus challenging the logic of the Cold War and deflecting charges that the movement was anti-American or pro-Soviet. The freeze movement brought the discussion of nuclear policy to the public square and democratized the debate about international security.

3.1 A Groundswell

The proposal gained momentum in the fall of 1980 when it was overwhelmingly approved in nonbinding referenda in western Massachusetts in local districts that in the same election voted for Reagan. The unexpected bipartisan support for the freeze electrified activists, and the new movement quickly swept across the country like a populist prairie fire. In 1982 similar initiatives in favor of the freeze were placed on the ballot in ten states, winning approval in all but one, and were approved in twenty-nine cities and counties (Maar, 2021, p. 113). A quarter of the US electorate, 18 million people, voted on nuclear freeze ballot initiatives that year, with 60 percent voting in favor. Resolutions in favor of the freeze were approved by more than a hundred major professional and civic organizations, from the US Conference of Mayors to the American Nurses Association, including dozens of major trade unions (Solo, 1988, p. 66–67). It was endorsed by hundreds of town meetings in New England, 11 state legislatures and more than 200 city councils. The historic Central Park rally in 1982 confirmed the movement's popular appeal.

Opinion polls consistently found overwhelming support for the freeze proposition. From the moment pollsters began asking about the idea, approval ratings stood at 70 percent or more. This was a rare and unique experience for the peace movement. Activists introduced a bold new concept for international security that immediately became the subject of national polling and commanded broad public support. The concept itself, backed by waves of social mobilization, became a means of shaping policy.

The popularity of the freeze and the broad public support it received derived entirely from the initiative of the peace movement. Peace activists placed the issue on the agenda and succeeded in making it a theme of public conversation, creating a political climate conducive to arms reduction. Pam Solo (1988) wrote that the freeze movement "was a dazzling success at raising public awareness and setting the terms of the debate" (p. 66).

The Freeze Campaign had significant support from many constituencies, but none was more important than the religious community. Nearly every faith group in the US endorsed the freeze, and many issued congregational statements on its behalf. The 1983 pastoral statement of the US Catholic Conference of Bishops was particularly influential, described by George Kennan as "the most profound and searching inquiry yet conducted by any responsible collective body into the relations of nuclear weaponry, and indeed of modern war in general" (Kennan, 1983). The bishops' letter attracted widespread press coverage, in part because the White House tried to convince the prelates to alter their statement and to tone down their criticisms of administration policies. The bishops did not explicitly endorse the freeze proposition, but they used the same language in calling for "immediate bilateral agreements to halt the testing, production and deployment of new nuclear weapons systems." A freeze by another name.

Religious constituencies historically have provided many benefits to the peace movement. They draw attention to the moral issues that motivate antiwar activism, especially the imperative to save lives. They offer organizational capacity and networks of potential supporters, along with the ability to reach mainstream audiences. The participation of churches and other religious bodies casts a mantle of respectability over peace and disarmament campaigns, giving legitimacy to the collective effort.

The mass mobilization for the freeze was rooted in growing public awareness of and concern about the threat of nuclear war. These concerns were enflamed by the Reagan administration's fire-breathing rhetoric about confronting the Soviet Union and possible use of nuclear weapons. Secretary of State Al Haig suggested the option of using nuclear weapons in Europe for "demonstrative purposes," a nuclear warning shot. Reagan told reporters "I could see where you could have the exchange of tactical weapons against troops in the field without it bringing either one of the major powers to pushing the button" (Maar, 2021, pp. 48–49).

The fear and consequences of nuclear war were underscored in a series of professional medical conferences organized by Physicians for Social Responsibility (PSR), one of the principal sponsors of the Freeze Campaign. More than thirty medical conferences on the effects of nuclear war took place in the early 1980s, most of them co-sponsored by prominent medical schools and state medical societies, which gave scientific validation to the presentations and enabled professionals in attendance to earn continuing education credits. In Los Angeles 2,900 people participated, and in Salt Lake the crowd numbered 2,000 (Cortright, 1993, pp. 28–33).

In nearly every city where the conferences were held, PSR sponsored extensive media campaigns, including a graphic image of the effects of a one-megaton bomb exploding over the local city, with concentric circles depicting the level of lethality emanating out from ground zero, where nearly everyone within a mile radius would perish, to distant suburbs where substantial parts of the population would be injured and contaminated with high levels of radiation. Local and regional media gave extensive coverage to these images and messages.

This was a classic example of earned media, the process of sponsoring events that attract widespread news coverage and enable movements to communicate their messages without large media budgets. Earned media is essential to the success of the peace movement and an important ingredient in efforts to alter public opinion. It is a key avenue of influence through which movements have been able to alter public opinion and win political support for peace initiatives.

The political effects of the freeze were evident in the government's response to the movement. The Reagan administration's initial policy agenda called for accelerating the arms race and expanding the US nuclear arsenal. The White House condemned the freeze proposal and mounted press campaigns to counter the statewide ballot initiatives. As public enthusiasm for the proposition spread, however, and political support for the idea mounted on Capitol Hill, the administration recognized it had to respond. The White House toned down its bellicose rhetoric and promised to negotiate with the Soviet Union for arms reduction. The administration abandoned its nuclear saber-rattling and adopted messages of moderation and support for arms control. All of this occurred before Gorbachev came to power. The change in the Reagan administration's approach to nuclear policy was the result of the influence of the freeze movement. (Wittner, 2003, p. 403).

3.2 The Freeze Goes to Washington

The Nuclear Weapons Freeze Campaign was primarily a grassroots organization with a mission of supporting statewide and local freeze groups. Initially, the campaign did not plan to engage in legislative action, hoping to establish a base of political support in local congressional districts before entering the fray of institutional politics. Many freeze activists wanted to steer clear of the legislative process in Washington. The dramatic success of the 1982 ballot initiatives, however, propelled the issue onto the national political agenda, attracting the support of members of Congress and presidential candidates. Despite its initial intentions, the Freeze Campaign found itself drawn into an unplanned and frustrating congressional debate on a nonbinding freeze resolution.

Many freeze activists were skeptical of congressional politics in principle, and their doubts deepened as they saw the muddled language of the legislation being introduced in Congress. In place of the movement's original call for an immediate halt to the arms race, the language of the measures debated in Congress merely urged the president to decide "when and how" to adopt a bilateral freeze. The legislative language became steadily more contorted and contradictory as qualifying amendments were added and new versions of the resolution were introduced by various members of Congress.

The result was a labyrinthine legislative process in which numerous qualifications and caveats were added to what was originally a clear call for an immediate halt to the arms race. The language in the resolution ballooned from a simple 16-line statement in the original version to a 152-line monstrosity 15 months later. The freeze resolution was approved by the House of Representatives in May 1983 by a lopsided 278–149 margin, but the legislation as adopted was practically devoid of meaning. Representative Leon Panetta (D-CA) told his colleagues during the debate, "whether you are a hawk or a dove … you can interpret anything you want in this resolution" (Cortright, 1993, p. 24). The freeze proposition was thus sacrificed to political expediency and linguistic obfuscation. The nonbinding resolution had no substantive impact on the continuing nuclear buildup.

Adoption of the freeze resolution nonetheless had symbolic political significance (Waller, 1987). News of the House approving the nuclear freeze conveyed the impression that the government was shifting its position and adopting the movement's proposal. The Reagan administration viewed the resolution as a threat to its nuclear policies and campaigned vigorously against it, which gave the freeze issue greater weight and had the unintended effect of boosting the movement's political standing. The Senate rejected the measure, and the US government never officially approved the resolution, but the vote brought further attention to the dangers of the arms race and attracted support for the freeze.

The inability to obtain formal government approval of the freeze resolution does not mean that the freeze movement failed. Peace movements rarely achieve their stated objectives, but by applying political pressures they can shift government policy preferences toward arms reduction and international cooperation. This was a key success of the freeze movement (Knopf, 1998, pp. 50–51).

On balance, House passage of the resolution was a plus for the movement. Legislative politics, rather than weakening the movement as some activists feared, brought greater media attention and grassroots engagement, increasing national recognition of the freeze in a positive feedback loop. Institutional and grassroots politics complemented each other.

As the 1984 presidential elections approached, the freeze movement was at the height of its popularity, with continuing strong approval ratings and a vast network of politically active grassroots supporters across the country. The movement had a proven ability to attract voter support in state and local referenda. Given that track record, it was no surprise that Democratic Party candidates sought to ride the coattails of the popular movement.

All the major Democratic contenders that year endorsed the freeze. Senator Alan Cranston (D-CA) was an early favorite of freeze activists, but he dropped out early after disappointing results in the Iowa and New Hampshire voting. The strongest peace candidate was Rev. Jesse Jackson, who placed third in both races, but his campaign did not take off that year as it did in 1988. Senator Gary Hart (D-CO) ran a strong campaign and won many primaries as a supporter of the freeze. He and Walter Mondale jousted over who would be the strongest champion of the freeze, with the former vice president prevailing to become the party's nominee.

Many freeze activists attended the Democratic Convention that year as delegates and won passage of a platform statement fully endorsing the freeze. It was the strongest platform statement against the nuclear arms race ever adopted by the party. The Freeze Campaign formed a political action committee, Freeze Voter, which mobilized thousands of local volunteers to support Mondale and help pro-freeze candidates in congressional elections.

When Mondale went down to defeat, some interpreted it as a loss for the freeze movement. Historian Henry Maar (2021) claimed that Reagan's victory caused "irreparable damage" to the Freeze Campaign, which was left "smoldering in the ashes" of Mondale's defeat (pp. 207–208). Certainly, the results were a political setback for the Democratic Party and a disappointment for activists who worked on the presidential race, but the electoral campaign had a deeper, more hopeful meaning for the movement.

Although the White House continued to oppose the freeze resolution, Reagan won the election in part by coopting the freeze message and portraying himself as a peace candidate. In his 1984 State of the Union message he famously declared "a nuclear war cannot be won and must never be fought." In his address to the United Nations that September he delivered a message of moderation and called for the superpowers to "approach each other" for the sake of world peace. He met for a cordial visit with Soviet Foreign Minister Andrei Gromyko right before the election. As Freeze Campaign coordinator Randy Kehler observed, "the Ronald Reagan elected in 1984 was quite different from the Ronald Reagan of 1980" (Maar, 2021, p. 207). Reagan traded his Cold War posture for a promise of peace. The freeze movement helped to create a political climate conducive to arms reduction, and Reagan adjusted his sails accordingly.

The direct results of peace movement electoral engagement in 1984 were limited, especially compared to the dramatic impact of the Dump Johnson campaign in 1968 and the Iraq antiwar electoral mobilization that flipped Congress in 2006 and helped to propel Obama to the White House. The freeze movement's involvement in 1984 was less direct but was nonetheless important, fashioning a new political agenda that Reagan coopted by toning down his rhetoric and promising arms control. Movements can influence political outcomes even with limited direct electoral engagement.

3.3 Winning Legislative Victories

The Nuclear Freeze Campaign organization faltered after the disappointing freeze debate in Congress and the 1984 elections, but the nuclear disarmament movement as a whole continued to grow and remained politically active. The plethora of organizations and coalitions that emerged nationally and in many states and local communities in the first half of the decade remained active. The momentum of the freeze movement continued and became more focused on achieving policy change as activists turned to legislative campaigns to begin implementing the freeze agenda. The movement became more adept at shaping the debate and leveraging its considerable grassroots power to influence legislative votes.

It was during the legislative fight for the freeze and the battle against the MX missile that the Monday Lobby Group was formed. This was a weekly gathering of peace and nuclear policy groups and congressional staff that became a coordinating center for disarmament and arms control legislative efforts on a range of Pentagon spending and nuclear security issues. The arms control lobby developed into a formidable presence on Capitol Hill. It had influence primarily because of its ability to activate a highly responsive network of grassroots activists in many states and hundreds of districts across the country.

The impact of this national network increased and showed up in numerous legislative fights over nuclear policy and weapons systems. Arms control lobbyists coordinated legislative advocacy messages with activists at the local level, who used that information to apply pressure on their elected members of Congress. The result was growing momentum on Capitol Hill to restrain the nuclear buildup.

The continued impact of the freeze movement was particularly evident in legislative debates in 1986. This was the time of the high watermark in membership growth for organizations such as SANE, the Council for a Livable World and others, with tens of thousands of people across the country willing to take action to support lobbying efforts against the arms race (Cortright, 1993). The House of Representatives that year adopted measures to curtail nuclear testing, limit the testing of antisatellite weapons, and cut funding for the Strategic Defense Initiative and the overall military budget, a string of successes described as an arms control "grand slam" (Congressional Quarterly Almanac, 1986, p. 478). Not all of these amendments made it through the legislative process to become law, but the votes reflected the impact of the movement and sent a message to the White House that legislators and their constituents wanted more vigorous action to bring the arms race to a halt.

The movement's infrastructure of grassroots activism and arms control lobbying were essential for the most sustained political fights of that era: the campaign to stop the MX missile and the campaign to halt nuclear testing. The MX and test ban campaigns successfully paired grassroots actions with political pressure in Washington to win important victories for the disarmament movement. They demonstrated the influence of mass participation at the grassroots level for achieving policy change.

3.4 Stopping the MX

The battle against the MX was the most extensive political fight of the disarmament movement during that era. The campaign had direct effects in curtailing a key component of the nuclear buildup and also had the indirect effect of motivating congressional efforts to demand progress in arms control negotiations. It spurred the creation of a diverse and effective coalition against the missile system and the refinement of targeted grassroots lobbying efforts.

The MX missile program was a monstrosity, the largest weapons system in the nuclear buildup. The original plan, developed in the latter years of the Carter administration and continued as a centerpiece of the Reagan nuclear agenda, called for building 200 new mobile Intercontinental Ballistic Missiles (ICBMs), each capable of carrying ten nuclear warheads, deployed in a massive basing system in the Great Basin of Utah and Nevada covering 25,000 square miles, five times the size of Connecticut (Rose, 2022). While commentators mocked the scale of the proposal, the White House, the Air Force and arms contractors were deadly serious about the plan and launched a major lobbying campaign on its behalf.

SANE and many other groups made stopping the new missile a priority. The campaign had two phases, the fight against the mobile basing system starting in 1979, and the legislative battle against the missile itself which stretched into 1985. In the initial phase, peace advocates, environmentalists, religious groups, taxpayer organizations, trade unions, Native American communities, ranchers, farmers and other local and national partners came together to mobilize opposition to the missile deployment plan in the Great Basin. It was a diverse coalition, bringing together a wide range of unusual partners who did not agree on many things but were united in their determination to stop the MX – a dramatic illustration of the importance of cross-constituency alliances in achieving political change.

The decisive voice in the region was that of the Church of Latter-day Saints, headquartered in Utah. In May 1981 the Church spoke out against the nuclear arms race and declared its opposition to the deployment of a "mammoth weapons system capable of destroying much of civilization" (1981; Prochnau, 1981).

The Morman statement and the growing opposition in the region killed the basing plan. The Reagan administration formally canceled the mobile missile system in October 1981. For the MX coalition, it was a landmark victory. Derailing the basing plan was only the first step, however, and a relatively easy one compared to the more challenging task of stopping the new missile system. Halting the basing system saved the Great Basin from environmental ruin, but the threat to international security posed by the new missile remained.

The campaign against the MX shifted its focus from cooperation with local partners in Utah and Nevada to working with arms control supporters on Capitol Hill. The campaign pivoted from local grassroots action in the Great Basin to national political action. The momentum gained in defeating the basing system carried over into the fight against the missile itself. A protracted legislative battle ensued in Washington and in legislative districts across the country as SANE, the Council for Livable World, the Coalition for a New Foreign Policy and other national groups mounted a legislative fight in Congress to cut funding for the missile. When the venerable citizen lobbying organization Common Cause entered the fray, the legislative campaign acquired additional sophistication and political heft. Working closely with the leadership of the House of Representatives and senior members of the Armed Services Committee, the coalition gradually succeeded in winning passage of amendments to cut the number of missiles, first in half and ultimately to just fifty weapons, as determined in a final compromise vote in 1985.

The legislative campaign against the MX became the dominant arms control issue in Congress, as dozens of climactic votes on missile funding occurred from 1982 through 1985. It was a classic David versus Goliath scenario, a growing but relatively small number of disarmament lobbyists aligned against legions of 'congressional liaison' officers from the Pentagon and major weapons contractors. The peace lobbyists had their own army of supporters, not in Washington but at the grassroots level, as many thousands of committed activists urged their congressional representatives and senators to vote against the missile.

The anti-MX coalition lost many of the major congressional votes, but it won often enough to stay in the legislative game and over the course of several years was able to whittle down the missile program to one-quarter of its original scale. It was not a complete success, but it was a substantial victory that reduced the scale of the threat posed by the new missile.

3.5 Single Issue, Multiple Impacts

Some in the broader disarmament movement questioned the value of campaigning against a single weapons system rather than challenging the entire nuclear buildup. The point of the freeze proposition was precisely to halt the development of all nuclear weapons, not just a single weapon. There was no contradiction between the two efforts, however. SANE and other groups in the Stop MX coalition also supported the nuclear freeze. The MX campaign was a way of focusing pressure on a particularly dangerous part of the nuclear buildup, one that was also politically vulnerable because of its massive environmental footprint and the dangers it posed to international security.

One of the principles of strategy as taught by Gene Sharp (2005) and others is to focus on objectives that are clear and achievable within a realistic time frame (Ackerman & Kruegler, 1994). Success in a specific campaign can motivate and empower activists and build momentum and organizational capacity to address larger strategic objectives. The MX issue fits that description as an example of low-hanging fruit. It was a Rube Goldberg scheme that was ripe for attack and might collapse of its own weight, especially if given a push by a well-organized citizen lobby. For the disarmament movement of the 1980s, focusing on the MX was a way of winning an important fight, strengthening coalitions and networks, and establishing the basis for a broader challenge to the entire arms race.

The MX campaign also served as a proving ground for enhanced methods of citizen lobbying in the local districts of key legislators. The ability of lobbyists from SANE and other groups to gain access to decision-makers in Washington depended on the extent of constituent pressure and press attention they generated in local districts. The coalition gained that attention by demonstrating the ability to activate hundreds or even thousands of registered voters from a legislator's home state or district on short notice for a specific legislative proposal. Activists also turned heads by attracting press coverage and media attention in local congressional districts. Backed up by a formidable presence at the local level, the representatives of the Washington-based groups were able to exert influence in Congress.

The campaign had the serendipitous effect of redirecting grassroot pressure on legislators against the MX into congressional pressure on the White House to negotiate for arms control. After the Reagan administration suffered a major defeat on the missile program in late 1982, Representatives Al Gore (D-TN), Senator William Cohen (R-ME) and other legislators developed the idea of conditioning their support for the missile on a more serious White House commitment to arms negotiations. In essence they traded the MX for arms control. It was a bizarre formulation that disarmament supporters rejected, but it had significant influence on the White House (Talbott, 1985, p. 217). By late 1983 the administration was forced to accept congressional proposals for a new more flexible US approach to negotiations (Talbott, 1984, pp. 609–610).

Grassroots demands on Congress against the MX generated pressure on the White House to moderate its previously hardline stance against arms control. One can argue whether the change in policy was meaningful (negotiations remained largely deadlocked until Gorbachev arrived on the scene), but the process was clearly a direct response to the anti-MX campaign and the power of grassroots lobbying against the arms race. It was an important example of the ways peace and disarmament activists can generate unintended but in this case positive effects on policy making by leveraging grassroots action to influence institutional politics.

3.6 Halting Nuclear Tests

In the wake of the frustrating 1983 freeze vote in the House of Representatives, activists within the freeze movement sought to go beyond merely symbolic measures to the actual implementation of a nuclear freeze. The "quick freeze" strategy, they called it, focused on halting nuclear weapons testing. The test ban was the priority because it was assumed that an inability to test would cut off the development and possible use of nuclear weapons. The proposed ban on nuclear weapons testing became a primary focus of activist attention over the following years.

The test ban campaign received a major boost in August 1985 when Gorbachev commemorated the fortieth anniversary of the bombing of Hiroshima by announcing a unilateral Soviet moratorium on nuclear weapons testing. SANE and the Freeze Campaign jumped on the issue and called for the US to reciprocate the Soviet moratorium. They launched a nationwide petition campaign for a bilateral US and Soviet testing moratorium. The petition drive was successful in gaining more than a million signatures in just three months, an impressive accomplishment in pre-Internet days. Boxes of signed petitions were delivered in person to Gorbachev by a delegation of activists from SANE, the Freeze Campaign and other US and European peace groups at the Reagan-Gorbachev summit in Geneva, Switzerland in November 1985.

Arms control groups also made the test ban a top legislative priority. Representative Ed Markey (D-MA) developed the concept of a "legislative reciprocal arms control initiative," an independent act of US nuclear restraint if the Soviet Union reciprocated in a verifiable manner. A US testing moratorium in response to Gorbachev's initiative would be a way to test the strategy. Markey introduced legislation in 1986 to suspend the funding of US nuclear test explosions above one kiloton. The measure won wide backing and swept through the House by a vote of 234 to 155 in August. A parallel bill was introduced in the Senate by Senators Mark Hatfield (R-OR) and Ted Kennedy (D-MA), but it failed to gain a majority (Wittner, 2003, pp. 387–388).

Grassroots organizers and arms control legislators in Congress kept up the pressure against nuclear testing. In 1986 activists formed a new group, American Peace Test (APT), which focused on mobilizing mass nonviolent civil disobedience at the Nevada Test Site near Las Vegas, where the US had been testing nuclear weapons since 1951. The goal was to bring thousands of people to Nevada to trespass at the site and physically obstruct the continuation of testing.

The impetus for APT came from Oregon Peaceworks, one of the major statewide peace and disarmament groups within the Freeze Campaign. Peaceworks organizers reached out to activists across the country to join the trek to Nevada and engage in civil disobedience to prevent further testing. Many people answered the call. During a series of protests at the test site from 1985 through 1988, more than 13,000 people were arrested. I was one of them, along with Freeze Campaign director Jane Gruenebaum. Also participating in civil disobedience in Nevada were celebrities such as American top forty radio DJ Casey Kasem and physicist Carl Sagan. Religious leaders Jim Wallis of Sojourners and William Sloane Coffin of SANE/Freeze also came to be arrested.

The Oregon Peaceworks strategy included working to elect members of Congress who would support the freeze and work for a test ban. When the congressional seat in their local Salem district opened up, they persuaded Mike Kopetski, a local legislator, to run for the position and promised to work for his election. They also asked him to join the protests at the test site. Kopetski made the trip to Nevada and came away from the experience more knowledgeable about nuclear weapons issues and convinced of the urgency of halting nuclear tests. Kopetski narrowly lost his race in 1988 but ran again in 1990 and won a solid victory, thanks in large part to the support of local environmentalists and peace activists. He vowed to go to Washington to help lead the fight against the arms race.

The legislative fight to halt funding for nuclear explosions had continued with partial successes for several years. In 1987 and 1988 the House of Representatives approved measures cutting funds for nuclear weapons testing, although the Senate again failed to go along. The administration of President George H.W. Bush was adamantly against a test ban. In 1991 the White House announced an aggressive program of additional underground nuclear testing, with several explosions planned over the following years.

Kopetski had a reputation as an effective legislator and coalition builder, and he put those skills to work in assembling a broad lineup of support for an amendment, modeled on previous legislation approved in the House, mandating a twelve-month moratorium on US nuclear tests. He scored a significant success when he convinced Democratic leader Richard Gephardt to cosponsor the bill, which was introduced in the fall of 1991. With SANE/Freeze and other disarmament and religious groups mobilizing constituent pressure across the country, the bill easily won passage in the House.

Winning support in the Senate remained a challenge. Kopetski's Oregon colleague Mark Hatfield led the Senate fight in cooperation with Democratic Majority Leader George Mitchell (D-ME), a new bipartisan combination that broke the previous deadlock and helped to gain majority support. When the

White House threatened to veto the measure, Senate sponsors of the bill broadened the coalition by lining up hawkish Democratic Senator James Exxon from Nebraska to support the bill. A revised bill was drafted that established a moratorium for nine months rather than a year, but it called for ending all testing after 1996 and included a mandate for negotiations to achieve a test ban treaty. The measure passed by a lopsided 68–26 vote, and the House agreed to the Senate bill. For the first time both houses of Congress approved legislation to halt nuclear testing (Wittner, 2003, pp. 439–441).

President Bush attacked the legislation, claiming it would undermine US security. He could not afford to veto it, however. Congressional sponsors had cleverly attached the measure to the energy and water appropriations bill, which included $500 million in funding for a super collider project in Bush's home state of Texas. Facing a veto-proof margin in Congress, the president reluctantly signed the bill on October 2, 1992. Disarmament activists and arms control legislators cheered. The fight to halt nuclear testing, which began in 1985 and was sustained through years of grassroots activism, civil disobedience and legislative lobbying, had finally achieved success.

Nuclear testing remained a hot issue in the following years, as citizen movements and governments in many countries worked to achieve a comprehensive nuclear test ban treaty. In July 1993 President Bill Clinton announced that the US would extend the nine-month testing moratorium imposed by the legislation and pursue global negotiations for a halt to all nuclear explosions. In that brief period of friendly US–Russia relations in the aftermath of the Cold War, negotiations proceeded smoothly and agreement was reached for a Comprehensive Test Ban Treaty (CTBT).

When Clinton tried to win Senate ratification for the CTBT, however, he ran into a wall of politically motivated Republican Party opposition. The Senate refused to ratify the agreement, with only forty-eight votes in favor, far short of the constitutional requirement of a two-thirds vote for Senate ratification.

The US did not become an official party to the CTBT, but the agreement gained nearly universal international support. It remains functional today as a de facto global nuclear testing moratorium despite the worsening of East-West security relations. The International Monitoring System established by the treaty maintains a rigorous network of 321 stations and 16 laboratories in 89 countries to detect potential violations of the treaty. The CTBT has been signed by 186 countries and embodies a global consensus against nuclear explosions, helping to sustain what has been described as a virtual taboo against nuclear testing (Kimball, 2023, p. 3).

4 Impacts of the Vietnam Antiwar Movement

The movement against the war in Indochina was the largest, most sustained and intensive antiwar campaign in American history. For a decade, as the US war escalated, reached its furious peak, and then gradually diminished, millions of citizens in the United States and around the world campaigned to bring the war to an end. During that era, as Tom Hayden (2017) wrote, "Americans took to the streets in numbers exceeding one hundred thousand on at least a dozen occasions, sometimes reaching half a million" (p. 19).

From the first major protests and teach-ins in 1965, to the Indochina Peace Campaign against funding the war in the 1970s, opponents of the war engaged in public education campaigns, mass marches, picketing, prayer vigils, boycotts, student strikes, draft resistance, legislative lobbying, media and advertising, electoral campaigns and more. Civil disobedience spread widely, reaching a peak in the Mayday action of 1971 when more than 12,000 people were arrested for attempting to shut down the city of Washington.

The antiwar movement had significant influence on government decision-making. As Carolyn Eisenberg (2023) concluded, "waves of mass demonstrations, accompanied by growing resistance inside the military, ongoing electoral activity, and lobbying efforts on Capitol Hill imposed significant constraints on presidential decision making" (p. 9). Antiwar action had definable impacts in restraining escalation and restricting military operations at several key turning points. Widespread draft resistance and growing disobedience in the ranks prompted government decisions that impeded the US ability to sustain the war.

In this section I look first at noncooperation with the draft and defiance within the armed forces and trace how these factors constrained the US ability to sustain the war. This is followed by an examination of the political challenges to Lyndon Johnson, the persistent waves of mass protest that confronted the Nixon administration and sowed the seeds of Watergate, and the lobbying campaign that finally halted funding for further war.

4.1 What if They Gave a War and Nobody Came?

During the Vietnam era millions of young men avoided military conscription by flocking to exempt occupations and schools, claiming phantom disabilities, or marrying early and having children. Hundreds of thousands actively resisted the draft as part of a vast movement that disrupted and began to cripple the conscription system. Approximately 170,000 obtained conscientious objector status (Tollefson, 1994). More than 40,000 draft resisters and deserters fled to Canada and Sweden. An estimated 570,000 young men were classified as draft offenders under federal law for failing to cooperate with the Selective Service

System (Tollefson, 1990, pp. 236–238). Of that number, charges were brought against 209,000, with 8,750 convicted and more than 3,200 imprisoned (Baskir & Strauss, 1978, p. 69). Protest actions and disruptions occurred at hundreds of Selective Service offices, with many incidents of obstruction and the destruction of draft records.

Antidraft organizers hoped to overwhelm the Selective Service System by filling the jails, but the White House chose not to prosecute most of the disobedients. Jailing thousands of additional draft resisters might have backfired and generated even wider youth unrest. The number of draft offenders was expanding "at an alarming rate," a senior adviser warned the Nixon administration, and the government was "almost powerless to apprehend and prosecute them" (Foley, 2003, p. 344).

Nixon had a novel solution to the problem of draft resistance. He called for abolishing conscription and creating an all-volunteer force. In his 1968 presidential campaign, Nixon said he would bring peace to Vietnam and establish a volunteer force to end the draft. It was a classic move of political opportunism, wrote historian Beth Bailey (2009), a bold stroke designed to attract the support of young voters and appeal to growing antiwar sentiment (p. 2).

Soon after taking office Nixon appointed a high-level commission to develop a plan for ending the draft. The resulting report argued that creating a volunteer force would avoid the high costs of "efforts to escape conscription." The Commission's econometric models described the resulting social and economic disruption as the greatest cost of the draft. The report also expressed concerns about mounting disaffection within the military. Ending conscription, it stated, would remove "troublemakers" in the ranks and ease the disciplinary problems then undermining military effectiveness (President's Commission, 1970, pp. 22, 32–33).

Promising to end the draft may have helped Nixon win the 1968 election, but it proved to be a nightmare for warmakers. The proposal was highly unpopular with military commanders. *Washington Post* reporters found that military offices had grave reservations about going all-volunteer (Johnson & Wilson, 1972). The same was true of the chairs of the Senate and House Armed Services Committees and other members of Congress. Nearly everyone in a position of authority within the military establishment was skeptical of the decision to go volunteer, Bailey observed. It was "a radical and unvetted" political campaign promise that had not been cleared with many senior military leaders or national security experts (p. 2).

The hawks worried that ending the draft would reduce military strength and make it impossible to continue fighting the war. They were right. Creating an all-volunteer force led to a sharp reduction in the size of the armed forces and had the effect of limiting US military options. Draft calls dropped sharply in

1969 and 1970 and reached zero at the end of 1972. Attempts to enlist a sufficient number of volunteers got off to a slow start, with each of the services failing to reach recruitment goals. The number of US service members fell from a peak of 3.5 million in 1968 to 2.3 million four years later. The size of the Army dropped nearly in half.

This massive drawdown of military strength was described by *Fortune* magazine as a "reluctant retrenchment" (Cameron, 1970). It was a unilateral reduction and contraction of military forces in the midst of a major land war, made without regard for the military operations and capabilities of the enemy. It was a politically motivated decision in response to draft resistance and antiwar pressure.

The goal of the antidraft movement was to end the war by depriving the Pentagon of the troops needed for battle. Few imagined this would happen through executive action to create a volunteer army, but the result was a significant success for the peace movement.

It is noteworthy that conscription has remained politically unpopular in the United States and was not reinstated for the Afghanistan and Iraq wars, placing a limit on the number of troops readily available for deployment, and requiring the mobilization of Reserve and National Guard forces to sustain military interventions.

4.2 Losing an Army

The Nixon administration continued to fight the war, but it also began a process of gradual troop withdrawal in response to antiwar pressure. The withdrawal policy was motivated by and contributed to the rise of dissent and resistance within the ranks. The GI peace movement emerged in 1968, well before the first troop withdrawals were announced in 1969. Hundreds of 'underground' antiwar papers were published at military bases, written by and for GIs, as the movement spread to all the services. Protests and petitions by service members occurred frequently, and absentee and desertion rates soared to record levels, peaking in 1971 (Carver et al., 2019; Cortright, 2005). Many soldiers continued to protest after leaving the military and joined with veterans returning from the war in the organization Vietnam Veterans Against the War (VVAW).

The 1971 absent without leave (AWOL) rate in the army was 17 percent, affecting one of every six soldiers, more than 70,000 absent GIs (Moser, 1996, p. 80). This deprived the military of approximately one million person-years of service, equivalent to half the total number of person-years of US troops in Vietnam that year. This had "an enormous impact on the ability of the armed forces to function" (Baskir & Strauss, 1978, p. 122.)

The mounting internal resistance led to a breakdown in military cohesion and capability, most strikingly evidenced in the growing number of combat refusals in Vietnam. According to former army combat commander Shelby Stanton, thirty-five incidents of combat refusal were recorded in the 1st Cavalry Division during 1970 (Stanton, 1985, p. 349). Some of the incidents involved entire units. If we extrapolate the experience of the 1st Cavalry to the other six army divisions in Vietnam at the time, it is likely that hundreds of mutinous events occurred during that year. An Army field team surveying small combat units in the spring of 1971 estimated that most companies had experienced one or two combat refusals over the previous six months (Sorley, 1999, p. 297).

The most horrifying evidence of the disintegration of the military was the spread of fragging, attacks against fellow soldiers with fragmentation grenades. The Army reported more than 550 fragging incidents in Vietnam from 1969 through 1971, resulting in 86 fatalities and over 700 injuries (McWethy, 1972, p. 22). George Lepre's study estimated that the total number of incidents was larger, ranging "from 600 to 850 or possibly more," including an estimated 100 to 150 fragging attacks in the Marine Corps (Lepre, 2011, p. 220). The targets of these attacks were mostly officers and noncommissioned officers (NCOs).

The leaders in charge of the armed forces at that time – Defense Secretary Melvin Laird and Senior Vietnam Commander General Creighton Abrams – were worried. Laird was an advocate for withdrawing troops and as morale among soldiers in Vietnam sank he argued for faster reductions. He recognized that the war was "destroying" the military, his biographer wrote, and saw his mission as "no less than the salvation of the US military" (Van Atta, 2008, p. 162). Senior officers who had previously requested more troops were now urging a quicker pullout. Abrams confided to an aide, "I need to get this Army home to save it" (Sorley, 1999, p. 289).

The decisions to end the draft and withdraw troops had a decisive impact on the outcome of the war. From 1969 onward, it was evident that the United States was heading for the exits and had abandoned the idea of achieving military victory. By 1970, if not before, US ground forces were in an advanced state of decay, with diminishing capacity and will for combat. As the air war intensified, resistance spread to the Navy and Air Force, with sabotage posing a significant threat to the Navy (Naval History and Heritage Command, 1973). Nixon tried to compensate for the lack of troops on the ground with massive US bombing, but he could not prevent defeat.

Many antiwar activists recognized the strategic significance of supporting GI dissidents. Civilian organizers helped to establish antiwar coffeehouses outside major military bases where soldiers could escape barracks life for a while and relax in a countercultural setting while learning about the antiwar movement (Parsons, 2017). Opponents of the war also established legal counseling programs for service members facing racial harassment and punishment for dissent.

The Pacific Counseling Service opened legal offices along the Pacific rim from Japan to the Philippines, and the Lawyers Military Defense Committee had an office in Saigon. These efforts helped to impede the war by providing material aid for service members who were increasingly defiant of military authority.

4.3 Challenging LBJ

For the antiwar movement as a whole, the main action strategy was to organize mass demonstrations as a form of indirect pressure on the warmakers. The purpose of the many actions nationally and locally was to shift public opinion against the war and challenge political decision-makers in Washington. As Lyndon Johnson continued to escalate the war despite the mounting protests, dissatisfaction within the Democratic Party spread and opponents of the war saw an opportunity to challenge the president electorally.

The president found himself confronted by antiwar protesters and excoriated by liberals who had previously supported him. A particularly dramatic confrontation occurred in Los Angeles in June 1967 when an unexpectedly large crowd of more than 10,000 nonviolent demonstrators disrupted his appearance. LA police forces attacked the protesters, causing a melee that left an indelible mark on the city and the president. Johnson rarely appeared in public after that (Reich, 1997).

Liberal groups launched an audacious campaign to unseat the war-making president. Americans for Democratic Action leader Allard Lowenstein joined with others to recruit thousands of student volunteers to support Minnesota Senator Eugene McCarthy as an antiwar candidate in the New Hampshire primary in March 1968. When the ballots were tallied, the little known challenger polled a remarkable 42 percent of the vote, compared to 49.5 percent for the president as a write-in candidate. McCarthy lost the vote count but won what historian Charles DeBenedetti (1980) termed "an astonishing psychological victory" that stunned Johnson and the political establishment in Washington (pp. 181–182). A few days later Sen. Robert Kennedy entered the Democratic primaries, a further blow to Johnson's reelection prospects. McCarthy and Kennedy together polled two-thirds of the vote in the twelve states with primaries that year.

These events unfolded as Americans were reeling from the shock of the February 1968 Tet Offensive, when Vietnamese liberation forces launched coordinated military attacks across South Vietnam. The televised scenes of mass carnage contrasted sharply with the rosy picture of military progress painted for the media a couple of months before by General William Westmoreland, senior commander in Vietnam, and Elsworth Bunker, US Ambassador in Saigon. The two leaders had been summoned to Washington for a public relations tour to counter the effects of the October 1967 March on the Pentagon, the largest antiwar action in Washington up to that time. A military officer later testified, "as the antiwar movement grew there was growing need to demonstrate success" (Small, 1988, p. 109). The Tet cataclysm burst the bubble of raised expectations, and public confidence in Johnson's conduct of the war plummeted.

The shocker came on March 31, 1968, two days before his looming defeat in the Wisconsin primary, when Johnson told a national television audience that he would not run for reelection and announced a bombing halt and the beginning of negotiations to end the war. The White House also rejected Westmoreland's request for 206,000 additional troops. The request for more forces included mobilizing 280,000 Reserve troops and increasing draft calls. In reviewing the request, the administration weighed multiple considerations, including the likelihood of greater antiwar resistance. Pentagon officials warned of growing disaffection, increased defiance of the draft and greater unrest in the cities. One spoke of the "gravest domestic risks" (Joseph, 1987, pp. 251–252).

Johnson's rejection of further escalation and pursuit of diplomacy was a major turning point in the direction of US policy. It ended the buildup of troops and opened the door to the possibility of a diplomatic solution. It would take several agonizing years for the United States to fully withdraw troops and negotiate a peace agreement, but this was the beginning of the end.

The dramatic events of 1968 showed the benefits of combining noninstitutional and institutional methods of political action. As draft resistance mounted, persistent large-scale street protests hounded the warmaking president and eroded his political base within the Democratic Party. Electoral challenges in the presidential primaries delivered a hammer blow to his reelection prospects and to the strategy for war.

Activists often debate whether the focus should be on street protest or political engagement, but it is not an either/or proposition. Both approaches are needed – generating pressure from the outside and engaging political institutions on the inside. The processes interact with each other and can be mutually reinforcing.

4.4 "The Movement and the 'Madman'"

When Nixon entered office and his administration continued the war, the peace movement responded with a massive wave of protest, including the Vietnam Moratorium on October 15, 1969, and the Washington Mobilization one month later.[2] The Moratorium campaign was initiated by veterans of the McCarthy

---

[2] Title from a documentary film of the same name, "The Movement and the 'Madman,'" PBS, *The American Experience*, Aired March 28, 2023, Produced and Directed by Stephen Talbot, www.pbs.org/wgbh/americanexperience/films/movement-and-madman/#cast_and_crew

campaign and had the support of a wide range of antiwar groups. The November march and rally were sponsored by the New Mobilization Committee to End the War in Vietnam, which was the successor to the radical coalitions that had organized previous national demonstrations (Koncewicz, 2024). The Moratorium concept was new and brought antiwar activism into the political mainstream. It was a call to pause business as usual on October 15 and engage in local action for peace. The idea caught on like wildfire and gained the endorsement of a wide range of organizations, trade unions, and many prominent intellectuals, artists and present and former government officials, as well as members of Congress. An estimated two million Americans participated in local activities that day, ranging from a gathering of 100,000 people on the Boston Common, to rallies and prayer vigils in hundreds of cities and towns. The Moratorium events were, in DeBenedetti's (1980) words, "the largest mass volunteer actions in American history" (p. 184). The November Mobilization was also massive, bringing an estimated half a million people to demonstrate at the Washington Monument and another quarter million in San Francisco. The rising tide of protest had a significant impact in preventing a major military escalation.

Nixon's supposed plan for ending the war turned out to be a threat of increased military pressure if Hanoi did not accept US terms for a negotiated peace agreement. He described the concept to his senior aide H.R. Haldeman (1978) as the "madman theory": a threat of massive military escalation against North Vietnam by an unpredictable president obsessed about communism "who has his hand on the nuclear button" (pp. 82–83, 98). Nixon instructed Henry Kissinger (1979) to pressure Hanoi to accept US terms or face a "decisive, savage blow" (pp. 284–285). To impress the Vietnamese and their Soviet supporters with its seriousness, the administration increased the operational readiness of US nuclear forces and placed nuclear-armed B-52 bombers on combat status (Sagan & Suri, 2003). The North Vietnamese were not intimidated, however, and called the president's bluff.

The game was up for Nixon, who feared he could not afford the political risks of carrying out the threatened escalation in the face of rising antiwar action. Kissinger (2003) had briefed Nixon in September that the "pressure of public opinion" would increase greatly in the following months (p. 586). Nixon (1978) admitted in his memoir that antiwar protests undermined his ultimatum to Hanoi: "these highly publicized efforts aimed at forcing me to end the war were seriously undermining my behind-the-scenes attempts to do just that" (p. 401). This was an admission that antiwar resistance prevented a major military escalation and constrained US military options. As Nixon wrote, "although I continued to ignore the raging antiwar controversy, I had to face the fact that it had probably destroyed the credibility of my ultimatum to Hanoi" (p. 403).

4.5 Seeds of Watergate

Nixon did not abandon his attempts to escalate military pressure, and in late April 1970, he sent US troops into Cambodia. The result was an angry explosion of protest, as students went on strike and many thousands of people poured into the streets in communities all over the country. On May 4 at Kent State University Ohio, National Guard troops fired into a crowd of unarmed demonstrators and killed four students. This sparked an even larger convulsion of protest. The national student strike that had started on May 1 spread rapidly, with walkouts recorded at 883 campuses (Early, 2020). At some universities, including Kent State, ROTC buildings were attacked and burned. National Guard units were mobilized in sixteen states. More than a hundred thousand people gathered a few days later in Washington and large numbers also demonstrated in San Francisco.

The furious public upheaval in response to Cambodia and Kent State prompted Congress to act. Many of the activists who protested near the White House also engaged in lobbying on Capitol Hill, pressuring legislators to force a withdrawal of troops. The Senate approved the Cooper-Church amendment cutting off funds for further ground operations in Cambodia. The White House had already withdrawn troops from Cambodia by the time the legislation was approved, but the stirring of congressional opposition was significant and became a factor in pressuring the administration to end the war.

The most ambitious attempt to end the war legislatively was the Hatfield–McGovern amendment to halt the funding of military operations in Vietnam, but it was defeated in the Senate in September 1970 by a vote of 55 to 39 (Smith, 1970). As public opinion turned against the war, however, congressional impatience with the war gradually increased, sending a message to the White House to continue bringing the troops home or face stronger legislative pushback.

The massive protests of November 1969 and May 1970 included some disruptive action and turned Washington into a "besieged city," said Kissinger (2003, p. 168). To get some sleep and avoid the protesters flooding the streets, he moved for a time from his apartment to the basement bomb shelter of the White House. He was joined there by other exhausted colleagues who were "unhappy, nearly panicked" (p. 170). Haldeman (1978) was among them. He later wrote that Nixon faced "unbearable pressures," which caused him "to order wiretaps and activate the plumbers [a secret break-in and dirty tricks squad] in response to antiwar moves" (p. 107). Kent State "marked a turning point for Nixon," wrote Halderman, "a beginning of his downward slide toward Watergate" (p. 121).

In 1971 the mass demonstrations were even larger, and they included an influential new voice, those who had served in the war. Vietnam veterans became a powerful constituency for the antiwar movement. In April of that year, eight hundred combat veterans and members of VVAW came to Washington DC for several days of action. They held protests at the Pentagon and other government agencies, marched to Arlington Cemetery to memorialize those killed in the war and lobbied members of Congress, where then Navy Lieutenant John Kerry testified before the Senate Foreign Relations Committee, asking "how do you ask a man to be the last man to die in Vietnam?"

The culmination of the VVAW program was a ceremony on April 23 in which hundreds of combat veterans, some in wheelchairs or on crutches, many wearing military fatigues, individually tossed their war medals and ribbons onto the steps of the US Capitol Building to denounce the war and declare their anger and distress at being decorated for serving in an unjust war.

The dramatic actions of the Vietnam veterans received front-page press coverage in national newspapers and were a lead story on network news broadcasts. The White House was panic-stricken. H. R. Haldeman complained that media coverage of the veterans was "killing us" and that the White House was "getting pretty well chopped up" by the press. Attorney General John Mitchell described VVAW as the most dangerous group in America. (Stacewicz, 1997, p. 336).

The VVAW actions were another decisive moment for the peace movement, a time when the American people turned more definitely against the war. (Hunt, 1999.) The veterans gave a brilliant political performance dramatizing the public demand for peace and convincing growing numbers of people to support immediate withdrawal. They drove Nixon crazy.

The web of criminality that ended Nixon's presidency was rooted in his paranoia about the peace movement. The White House took extreme measures to hide the truth about the war and counter antiwar narratives. Illegal wiretapping began in 1969 in response to leaks of information about the 'secret' bombing of Cambodia. The plumbers were activated in 1971 to discredit Daniel Ellsberg for releasing the Pentagon Papers. They burglarized the office of Ellsberg's psychiatrist in Los Angeles in search of incriminating information, a preview of their break-in at Democratic Party offices in the Watergate a year later. The purpose of the Watergate burglary, according to convicted conspirator James McCord, was to find information on links between the Democratic Party and VVAW based on false claims that VVAW was planning terrorist acts at the forthcoming Republican Party convention. (O'Sullivan, 2019, May 9). The administration's campaign against peace advocates and antiwar veterans contributed to the president's undoing. This was another indirect but significant effect of the mounting opposition to the war, an example of the peace movement helping to shape history in unexpected ways.

Protest action continued into 1971 and beyond. The constant mass marches became tiresome for some, but they were telegenic, and even thrilling as historian Melvin Small (2010) wrote (p. 544). They kept the demand "Out Now" in the public eye and were a necessary means of mobilizing opposition. Media coverage of the movement was often distorted, however. Television news tended to focus on images of violence and the extreme acts of a few rather than portraying the far greater number of peaceful protesters from all walks of life, including the religious community. "As the war steadily lost popularity in the late Sixties," Todd Gitlin (1987) observed, "so did the antiwar movement" (p. 262). The White House frequently disparaged the image of peace activists and branded protesters as unpatriotic extremists.

The major antiwar coalitions did little to counter these calumnies. They had minimal communication capacity and lacked a coherent strategy for conveying positive images and messages that could attract broader social support. The exception to this pattern was the Moratorium Committee. Its leaders Sam Brown and David Hawk were effective media spokespersons, and the Committee conveyed an inviting and inclusive message that avoided the theme of rebellious youth and tried to reach a cross-section of society. A Moratorium advertisement featured a father with a buzzcut embracing his long-haired son above the heading, "October 15th: Fathers and Sons Together against the War." (Robinson, 2023).

4.6 Defunding the War

Even as the last US ground troops were leaving Vietnam, the Nixon administration tried to stave off defeat through an intensification of bombing in Cambodia and by providing more weapons and money to its beleaguered client regimes in Saigon and Phnom Penh. Peace activists created the Indochina Peace Campaign, the Indochina Resource Center and the Coalition to Stop Funding the War to inform people about the air war and lobby Congress against further funding. The emphasis was on grassroots education and mobilization directed at decision-makers in Washington. A steady stream of telegrams, letters, lobbying visits and protests outside congressional offices pressured legislators to act.

These efforts paid off dramatically in June 1973 when Congress approved landmark legislation terminating all US military activity "in or over or off the shores" of Indochina (Belasco, 2007, p. CRS-6). The binding restriction went into effect on August 15, 1973. The war ended formally with the January 1973 Paris Peace Agreement, but bombing operations in Cambodia had continued. The congressional action marked the definitive end of all US military operations in Vietnam.

The next step for the movement was to halt the flow of funds to the Saigon regime, as large-scale military operations continued against communist-controlled territory in South Vietnam. In April 1974 the White House requested $1.6 billion in military aid for Saigon for the coming fiscal year. Congress voted it down and later that year appropriated less than half that amount (Veith, 2013, pp. 58, 61). The administration also requested $474 million in emergency supplemental aid for the existing fiscal year. The House rejected that request as well, and the Senate approved lessened supplemental aid a month later. These votes against military aid requests were a "serious Congressional setback" to the administration's plans to continue the war (Finney, 1974).

The final blow came in early 1975. As communist-led troops closed in on Saigon and Phnom Penh, President Gerald Ford attempted to prevent defeat by requesting additional military assistance for the faltering regimes. Three thousand activists gathered in Washington in January for an antiwar assembly and lobbying effort to block further aid. Graham Martin, the US ambassador in Saigon, cabled Washington to urge support for the funding, but his pleas fell on deaf ears. In March Congress rejected the requests, sealing the fate of the South Vietnamese and Cambodian governments, which fell a few weeks later.

Martin attributed Congress's decisions during this period to what he called "one of the best propaganda and pressure organizations the world has ever seen." His back-handed swipe was a grudging acknowledgment of the power of the antiwar movement. He credited the "beautifully orchestrated" work of the Indochina Resource Center. "I have watched these operations over the world for a long period of time," he later testified before Congress: "these individuals deserve enormous credit for a very effective performance." It was "the constancy of the drumming in day after day" and "the building of the pressure from the constituencies" that produced an "enormously effective" campaign to end US involvement in the war (Wells, 1994, pp. 576–577.)

The direct pressures applied by the antiwar lobby influenced congressional decisions to cut funding for the Saigon regime. The Watergate crisis also played a role, steadily eroding the administration's political position. So did the growing number of members of Congress who had been elected on an antiwar platform and were determined to end any further American involvement. These developments combined to reinforce the impact of antiwar activism. The role of the peace movement was decisive in maintaining a persistent drum beat of opposition over a period of ten years to end a war that many came to recognize never should have been fought.

The antiwar movement compelled the White House to disengage from Vietnam at a faster pace than many military commanders and national security officials would have preferred, Gregory Daddis (2017) concluded (p. 143). The state of public opinion and domestic politics were key variables in the strategic calculations of both the Johnson and Nixon administrations. Decisions about the war were based on assessments of antiwar opposition and its political impacts at home. This was "irrefutable evidence" of the movement's impact on policy-making, wrote Small (1988), a testament to the power of protest (p. 231).

As Eisenberg (2023) concluded, Nixon faced "significant constraints on his decision making, created by a vigorous antiwar movement, a restless Congress, and an impatient public" (p. 515). The cumulative impact of prolonged public opposition impeded the war effort and forced the withdrawal of troops and an end to US military operations. For the antiwar movement it was an extraordinary accomplishment, however long and difficult, which helped to change the course of history.

When the final end to the war came on April 30, 1975, many of those who had worked for years to end the fighting gathered spontaneously in public places. In Washington, DC, hundreds of us streamed into Lafayette Park in front of the White House where the first protest against the war had occurred a decade before. There was no program and no speeches. People just wandered about in small groups or alone, speaking softly, averting eyes, holding back tears in a collective mood of grief over the millions who had died, but also relief that the slaughter was finally over. Many felt a profound sadness that it had taken so long to bring the war to an end, and wondered whether wiser strategies and methods could have brought success sooner. It's an unanswerable question that haunts all antiwar movements.

5 Anti-nuke Deja-vu?

What lessons can be gleaned from the history of these movements, and how might they apply to the challenges of war and nuclear weapons today? Each of the movements was unique and occurred in a distinct historical setting, but they have certain characteristics in common. All were a response to overly militarized US foreign policies. They employed methods of mass protest, grassroots organizing, media communications and lobbying and electoral campaigns. They built coalitions with multiple groups and constituencies, especially religious communities.

Some of us participated in all three movements, each time building upon what we experienced in previous campaigns and connecting with new and old colleagues to organize anew. Along the way, through continuous study of movement history and the refinement of social mobilization methods, we applied knowledge about what was done correctly or not in the past to improve peace organizing today.

Below I offer observations, on what I consider essential factors for peace movement effectiveness, which are also applicable to social justice movements generally Success depends on the following:

- the ability to attract mass participation and show broad public support for movement demands
- a credible, widely shared critique of existing policies and the articulation of constructive alternatives
- visionary ideas and goals for the future, combined with concrete, achievable objectives for near-term policy campaigns
- engagement in instrumental politics, with an emphasis on the mobilization of grassroots support for legislative and electoral action
- effective communication and framing strategies that are grounded in the values and beliefs of targeted audiences and that attract support for movement demands
- the creation of broadly based coalitions, with significant participation from relevant religious communities and the involvement of women, people of color and affected constituencies
- realism in recognizing incremental policy changes as success, defending those gains when they come under attack and building on them for future achievement
- persistence and a commitment to the long haul

5.1 Nukes Redux

It may be useful to apply these lessons to the challenge of preventing a global arms race today. Nuclear dangers have increased significantly in recent years. The United States, Russia, China and other states are building new nuclear bombs and upgrading weapons delivery systems. Moscow has threatened repeatedly to use nuclear weapons during its aggression against Ukraine, amidst increased East-West tensions and the collapse of negotiated arms control. China is becoming more bellicose and is building additional nuclear weapons, although its estimated stockpile of 500 to 600 bombs is well below the total US and Russian arsenals of about 3,700 and 4,380 weapons respectively. North Korea now has an estimated fifty weapons and has enhanced its ballistic missile capacity. India and Pakistan continue to expand their arsenals and Israel maintains approximately ninety deliverable nuclear bombs (SIPRI, 2024).

In the United States programs are underway to improve and upgrade strategic weapons delivery systems and theater-range weapons. The US is adding more nuclear warheads and more nuclear-capable bombers and missiles. Development is underway on the new Sentinel land-based missile program, which will replace the current fleet of 400 Intercontinental Ballistic Missiles with a new force of more powerful ICBMs capable of firing multiple warheads. Production is underway on new nuclear-armed, air-launched cruise missiles, and Congress has continued funding for a new nuclear-armed, sea-based cruise missile system. The US is building two vast facilities for producing plutonium pits, the hollow spheres of plutonium that are compressed to cause nuclear explosions. The new bomb factories together are designed to produce eighty plutonium pits per year (Scoles, 2023, p. 39).

Republican members of Congress and former aides to Donald Trump have pushed for a resumption of nuclear testing (Broad, 2024). The stated purpose is to increase preparedness for the use of newly designed warheads. The renewal of testing would accelerate the emerging arms race and undo one of the signature achievements of the freeze movement. The testing and development of new bombs would increase the risk of nuclear weapons being used.

The growing nuclear danger has led to an increase in public awareness and concern. This is reflected in the success of the film *Oppenheimer*, the *New York Times* series "At the Brink" and Annie Jacobson's bestselling book, *Nuclear War: A Scenario*. To date, however, citizen activism on the nuclear issue has been insufficient. Many effective groups are working to increase public awareness of the nuclear danger, including Back from the Brink, Peace Action, the Arms Control Association, the Bulletin of Atomic Scientists and the 2017 Nobel-prize-winning International Campaign to Abolish Nuclear Weapons. These and related groups produce outstanding publications, are active on the web and in social media, and have sponsored petitions, statements and local action, but the levels of citizen participation so far are below what is necessary for political impact.

One of the challenges for nuclear activism today is the urgency of other major crises, such as climate change, the crisis in Gaza and threats to democracy. These concerns grab our attention and fill social media feeds. The crisis of a rapidly warming global climate is especially important. It is similar to the nuclear weapons danger in posing an existential threat to human life and the fate of the earth.

As Jonathan Schell (2007) wrote,

> The two perils have a great deal in common. . . . Both put stakes on the table of a magnitude never present before in human decision making. . . . Both require a fully global response. Anyone concerned by the one should be concerned with the other. It would be a shame to save the Earth from slowly warming only to burn it up in an instant in a nuclear war (p. 7).

There are other links between the two. As Neta Crawford (2022) has documented, the Pentagon is the single largest institutional energy consumer and producer of greenhouse gases in the world. Its emissions are greater than those of many countries. US military strategy and military deployments have largely focused on securing access to Middle East oil. War causes severe environmental damage, as is evident in Ukraine and Gaza, and a nuclear war would be a climate-altering ecological catastrophe.

5.2 A New Nuclear Freeze Movement?

What would it take to spark a new grassroots mobilization for nuclear sanity? An option under consideration by some activists is to launch a global campaign to stop the arms race. The goal would be to mobilize support for a public demand that the US and other countries stop building bombs and nuclear delivery systems. It would attempt to organize a mass public outcry that "we do not need or want more nuclear weapons."

The campaign would focus on a clear, easily understandable and short proposition that might attract broad popular support:

> We oppose the building of more nuclear weapons. We call on the leaders of the United States, Russia, China and other nuclear states to implement a mutual, verifiable halt to the development of new nuclear bombs and weapons systems. We urge negotiations for renewed arms reduction, to step back from the brink and achieve a world without nuclear weapons.

The campaign might begin at the grassroots level with public education events, tied to social action such as vigils and visits at congressional offices or other appropriate locations. It would have a social media component that asks, "do you want more nuclear weapons?," urging respondents to take action in their communities. If support builds at the local level, the proposition could be translated into legislation seeking a suspension of funding for building new nuclear weapons programs and urging the nuclear powers to negotiate steps for a mutual freeze and renewed arms reduction.

The initial educational materials could rely on the publications and products of existing disarmament groups. The themes would include denying the need for more nukes, debunking the theory of deterrence, and reminding citizens that nuclear weapons are suicidal. Any substantial use of these weapons could devastate the earth's biosphere and kill hundreds of millions of people (Savitsky, 2022).

The campaign messages would cite the Reagan–Gorbachev declaration, recently reiterated by the five legacy nuclear states, "a nuclear war cannot be won and must never be fought," and the consensus statement of world leaders at the 2022 Bali summit: "the use or threat of use of nuclear weapons is inadmissible" (White House, 2022).

The goal of the proposed campaign would be to spark greater public awareness of the growing nuclear danger and offer a clear policy pathway for reducing that threat. It would seek to build the constituency for freezing and reversing the arms race. It would support and enhance the work of existing groups by providing a common vehicle for all to use.

The campaign would start in the US as the most influential state and the country with the greatest media impact, but for the proposed global freeze it would be necessary to gain support in other countries, especially nuclear weapons states such as the UK, France, India, Pakistan and Israel. Independent civil action is unlikely in Russia, China and North Korea, but it might be possible to gain endorsement for the proposition from a few independent experts and former officials in those countries and to disseminate the message through available social media platforms. The campaign could also reach out to non-aligned countries and states allied to one or more of the nuclear powers to urge nuclear restraint and mutual steps toward arms reduction.

5.3 Questions for Movement Building

Some activists consider the idea of a freeze too limited. They insist that the goal should be nuclear abolition, with a focus on gaining support for the Treaty on the Prohibition of Nuclear Weapons (TPNW) adopted at the United Nations in 2017. The TPNW is indeed a landmark development that establishes nuclear abolition in international law and strengthens the legal architecture against nuclear proliferation. No nuclear weapons state has signed the agreement, however, and many major states, including the United States, are strongly opposed to the treaty. The TPNW embodies the strategic goal of nuclear abolition, but it is not a viable near-term policy objective in the United States.

Support for a no new nukes campaign doesn't mean abandoning disarmament. A world without nuclear weapons remains the goal of the peace movement. It is an aspiration that motivates many activists, including this author, but to reach beyond the choir of current disarmament activists more realistic political objectives are needed. To make progress toward nuclear abolition governments must stop making the danger worse. Halting the arms buildup is a necessary step toward the larger goal.

Some organizers worry about competition among existing groups, but a campaign that builds greater grassroots activism could benefit all. During the freeze movement of the 1980s, SANE and other groups experienced significant membership growth and income. At SANE we supported the freeze but also pursued other programs such as stopping the MX missile. A unifying agenda could enhance the programs of existing groups as they work in parallel to reduce the threat of an accelerating arms race.

In today's political climate, congressional legislation to suspend the funding of new nuclear weapons will not win many votes, at least not initially. The Arms Control Association and other groups in Washington, DC, are urging support for for legislation that recommends arms control dialogue and condemns Russia's threats of nuclear weapons use. Partial measures such as this fall far short of freezing the current buildup, but they provide a basis for community-based public education. Lobbying for resumed arms control dialogue could be a catalyst for coordinated local group actions in multiple communities.

As with all movements, a new campaign would require substantial media communications capacity and effective framing and delivery of messages. The clarity and feasibility of the proposed freeze-related proposal would be an asset, especially if it is framed in language and images that appeal to the broadly shared beliefs and values of targeted audiences. Patriotic images and themes would be essential, with references to the arms reduction leadership of Ronald Reagan and words of support for disarmament of other former presidents and senior military commanders.

The media campaign would need the legitimacy that comes from a diverse base of supporters, including those who form the backbone of movements on climate change, women's rights, LGBTQ activism and many other modern organizing efforts. It would also need credible endorsers and spokespersons among scholars and experts, especially scientists, and former diplomats and security officials. In December 2021, the Union of Concerned Scientists released a letter signed by nearly 700 scientists and engineers, including 21 Nobel laureates and 69 members of the National Academies, calling for limiting the role of nuclear weapons in US policy (Union of Concerned Scientists, 2021). Its recommendations included canceling the Sentinel ICBM program. The proposed campaign could build upon and expand this base of expertise and legitimacy.

Celebrities, artists and performers have supported peace and disarmament campaigns in the past and could play a constructive role again. A recent example of Hollywood engagement was the March 2024 open letter that was released on the eve of the Academy Awards ceremony. The project took advantage of the attention paid to the Oscar-winning film *Oppenheimer*. The letter was published as a full-page ad in the *LA Times*. It warned of current nuclear dangers and urged greater efforts to "make nukes history." Signatories included *Oppenheimer* cast members Tony Goldwyn and Matthew Modine, Oppenheimer's grandson, Charles Oppenheimer, screen stars Rosanna Arquette, Ellen Burstyn, Michael Douglas, Jane Fonda, Viggo Mortensen, Emma Thompson, and Lily Tomlin, and recording artists such as Jackson Browne, Annie Lennox and Graham Nash. It was accompanied by billboards in Los Angeles, videos on social media and an art installation at a popular LA shopping and restaurant complex (Nuclear Threat Initiative).

It was an effective publicity effort, but it did not catalyze sufficient public activism. The statement would have been more useful strategically if it had included a specific ask, for example asking readers and viewers to take action in their communities in support of measures to halt the development of new nuclear weapons.

The effectiveness of a new campaign will depend on building coalitions with other organizations and constituencies. The most effective campaigns are those with active, broadly based alliances that cross sectoral, political and social boundaries. Religious communities are often at the core of these formations. The voice of the religious community has been and remains a potent force in American affairs and is important for movements that work for peace.

The US Conference of Catholic Bishops and mainline Protestant dominations were opposed to the Iraq War and provided support for the goals of the freeze movement. They are likely to be sympathetic to a new global freeze proposal, although their social action capacities have diminished over the years. Catholic institutions devoted to charity, development and international peace recently experienced budget cuts. Jewish religious bodies were in favor of the original freeze and probably would favor the new initiative, although their attention remains focused on the tragedy in Israel and Gaza. Islamic organizations have not been active on nuclear issues in the past but might endorse the global freeze, although their attention is also fixed on the crisis in Palestine and the Middle East.

If religious participation at the national level is weaker than in the past, organizers can focus more on religious outreach at the local level, working with community-based congregations and grassroots religious alliances. This approach would align with the goal of building a base of support at the grassroots level.

Whether a new antinuclear initiative is feasible remains to be seen. The urgency of the nuclear danger is certain, as is the need for greater citizen awareness and mobilization, but the obstacles to creating a new campaign are many. The salience of nuclear issues has increased lately but is still low, while the urgency of other issues remains high. The prospects for breaking through in the media are uncertain.

The viability of a new campaign idea may depend on testing the proposition through local action, as organizers did in 1980 with the first nuclear freeze ballot initiatives in western Massachusetts. Back from the Brink has had success in gaining support for its broad denuclearization agenda, with endorsements from dozens of city councils and national and local elected leader. This is a solid base of support for building a campaign to stop the arms race (Back from the Brink, 2025). It will be up to local activists to refine the suggestions examined here and test their viability among potential supporters.

6 Conclusion

Building a movement to stop the arms race will be difficult in a world overflowing with deadly weapons and more on the way. In the United States, both Democrats and Republicans in Congress have been supportive of more military spending and building upgraded nuclear weapons systems. Few voices of dissent are raised against these policies. The obstacles to peace advocacy seem insurmountable. Yet progress toward denuclearization is possible and has occurred in the past at similar movements of peril. Forty years ago, during a comparable period of rising arms spending and East-West tensions, at much higher levels of nuclear overkill, history turned.

Who could have imagined then that the Berlin Wall would fall without a shot being fired and nuclear arsenals would be slashed by more than 80 percent? Transformational change is achievable and often begins with a push from civil society. Gorbachev and Reagan signed the treaties that ended the Cold War, but the freeze movement and disarmament campaigns of Europe prepared the way. Massive citizen pressure changed the climate of opinion and made support for arms reduction politically possible and then popular. The resulting policy change went beyond a freeze to a dramatic reversal of the arms race.

That victory ended the Cold War and led to a global sigh of relief. Fear of nuclear holocaust receded from public consciousness, and the salience of nuclear issues dropped. We stopped worrying about the bomb. Now we are in a very different era, facing new, more complicated and dangerous nuclear threats. In responding to the present peril we can draw inspiration and lessons from the experiences of the past.

As these sections indicate, activists can build movements if they articulate clear, focused and achievable demands and deliver messages that are understandable and likely to attract public support. Effective framing and digital messaging are essential. It is also necessary to take action in the streets and at educational institutions. The power of movements depends on the ability to mobilize mass participation, at the grassroots level and nationally. It also derives from the creation of broad and diverse coalitions, and the ability to engage with political institutions. The combination of these factors and the application of wise strategies can create change.

Organizing and sustaining peace movements is a long and arduous process. Tangible victories are few, and shifts in policy are often unrecognizable as they occur. Political opposition to the Iraq War did not stop the invasion, but it weakened the war effort and generated pressure for withdrawal. The nuclear freeze movement emerged from the grassroots to alter the terms of debate and reshape political culture. The Vietnam antiwar movement stretched over a decade to force the withdrawal of US troops and ultimately end the war.

Change often comes slowly and incrementally, with partial successes that fall short of larger goals. Small victories are nonetheless important and can lead to additional steps and through continuous pressure may produce substantive change. The grand visions of world peace and disarmament that inspire activist hopes are not realized, but movement pressures lead to steps in that direction. They make a modest contribution toward a safer, less violent world, at least for a while. The direction of history is not linear. Setbacks occur, as we are experiencing now, and activists face the challenge of revisiting past debates and formulating strategies to recover previous gains and renew progress toward sanity.

Realistic expectations are necessary. The goal of movements is not to create utopias or build a perfect society. The mission is to advance human progress, redress political grievances and make an imperfect world more tolerable and just. When movements succeed the gains are important, but many challenges remain and always will. The struggle continues. Campaigns for peace and justice are always necessary, and they can win, especially when activists are able to learn from and improve upon previous practices.

Movements need long-distance runners, those who are committed to the struggle for justice and peace in all seasons, regardless of the success or failure of a specific campaign. Fundamental change is usually a gradual and long-term process. Persistence and a commitment to the long haul are essential to achieving effective change.

References

Ackerman, S. (2021). *Reign of terror: How the 9/11 era destabilized America and produced Trump*. Viking.

Ackerman, P. & Kruegler, C. (1994). *Strategic nonviolent conflict: The dynamics of people power in the twentieth century*. Praeger.

Angle, M. (2007, July 12). Defying Bush, House passes new deadline for withdrawal from Iraq. *The New York Times*. https://archive.nytimes.com/www.nytimes.com/cq/2007/07/12/cq_3069.html.

Back from the brink. (2025, April). *Who's on board*. https://preventnuclearwar.org/whos-on-board/.

Bailey, B. (2009). *America's army: Creating the all-volunteer force*. Harvard University Press.

Baker, P. (2014). *Days of fire: Bush and Cheney in the White House*. Anchor Books.

Baskir, L. M. & Strauss, W.A. (1978). *Chance and circumstance: The draft, the war and the Vietnam generation*. Alfred Knopf.

Belasco, A. (2007, January 6). *Congressional restrictions on U.S. military operations in Vietnam, Cambodia, Laos, Somalia, and Kosovo: Funding and non-funding approaches*. (CRS Report No. RL 33803). https://sgp.fas.org/crs/natsec/RL33803.pdf.

Broad, W. (2024, July 5). Trump advisers call for U.S. nuclear weapons testing if he is elected. *The New York Times*. www.nytimes.com/2024/07/05/science/nuclear-testing-trump.html.

Calhoun, J. (1980, October). The Vietnam war and the Vietnam generation [Review of the book *Chance and circumstance: The draft, the war, and the Vietnam generation*, by L. M. Baskir and W.A. Strauss]. *Peace and Change*, 6(3). 71–77. https://doi.org/10.1111/j.1468-0130.1980.tb00421.x.

Cameron, J. (1970, November). The armed forces' reluctant retrenchment. *Fortune*, 82(5), 69–73, 166, 173–174.

Carver, R., Cortright, D., & Doherty, B. (2019). *Waging peace in Vietnam: Soldiers and veterans who opposed the war*. New Village Press.

Chenoweth, E. (2021). *Civil resistance: What everyone needs to know*. Oxford University Press.

The Church of Jesus Christ of Latter-day Saints. (1981, May 5). *First presidency statement on the basing of the MX missile*.

Congressional Quarterly Almanac. (1986). 99th Congress, 2nd Session. August 28, 2024 from https://library.cqpress.com/cqalmanac/toc.php?mode=cqalmanac-toc&level=2&values=1986+-+99th+Congress%2C+2nd+Session.

Cortright, D. (1993). *Peace works: The citizen's role in ending the Cold War.* Westview Press.

Cortright, D. (2005). *Soldiers in revolt: GI resistance during the Vietnam War.* Haymarket Publishers.

Cortright, D. (2023). *A peaceful superpower: Lessons from the world's largest antiwar movement.* New Village Press.

Cramer, J.K. (2007). Militarized patriotism: Why the U.S. marketplace of ideas failed before the Iraq War. *Security Studies, 16*(3). 489–524. https://doi.org/10.1080/09636410701547949.

Crawford, N. C. (2022). *The Pentagon, climate change and war: Charting the rise and fall of U.S. military emissions.* MIT Press.

Daddis, G. A. (2017). *Withdrawal: Reassessing America's final years in Vietnam.* Oxford University Press.

Davis, M. (2007, January–February). The Democrats after November. *New Left Review, 43.* 5–31.

DeBenedetti, C. (1980). *The peace reform in American history.* Indiana University Press.

Early, S. (2020, April 24). Fifty years ago this spring, millions of students struck to end the war in Vietnam. *Jacobin.* www.jacobinmag.com/2020/04/kent-state-shooting-vietnam-war-protest-student-organizing.

Eisenberg, C. W. (2023). *Fire and rain: Nixon, Kissinger, and the wars in Southeast Asia.* Oxford University Press.

Elsea, J., Garcia, M., & Nicola, T. (2008, February 27). *Congressional authority to limit U.S. military operations in Iraq.* (CRS Report No. RL33837).

Everts, P.P. (1989). Where the peace movement goes when it disappears. *Bulletin of Atomic Scientists, 45*(9), 26–30. www.tandfonline.com/doi/abs/10.1080/00963402.1989.11459746.

Finney, J. W. (1974, May 7). Senate rejects rise in arms aid to South Vietnam. *The New York Times.* www.nytimes.com/1974/05/07/archives/senate-rejects-rise-in-arms-aid-to-south-vietnam-action-led-by.html.

Foley, M.S. (2003). *Confronting the war machine: Draft resistance during the Vietnam War.* University of North Carolina Press.

Gamson, W. (1990). *The strategy of social protest.* (2nd ed.). Wadsworth.

Gitlin, T. (1987). *The sixties: Years of hope, days of rage.* Bantam Press.

Godfroy, J. F., Powell, J. S., Morton, M. D., & Zais, M. M. (2019). Surge and withdrawal 2007–2011. In J. Rayburn & F. Sobchak (Eds.), *The U.S. Army in the Iraq War* (pp. 619–641) (Vol. 2). U.S. Army War College Press.

Gordan, Philip H. (2020). *Losing the long game: The false promise of regime change in the Middle East.* St. Martin's Press.

Haldeman, H. R. (1978). *The ends of power.* Times Books.

Hayden, T. (2007). *Ending the war in Iraq*. Akashic Books.

Hayden, T. (2017). *Hell no: The forgotten power of the Vietnam peace movement*. Yale University Press.

Hays, C. (2008, July 16). MoveOn.Org is not as radical as conservatives think. *The Nation*. www.thenation.com/article/archive/moveonorg-not-radical-conservatives-think/.

Healy, P. (2006, August 8). Lamont defeats Lieberman in primary. *The New York Times*. www.nytimes.com/2006/08/08/nyregion/08cnd-campaign.html.

Heaney, M. T., & Rojas, F. (2015). *Party in the street: The antiwar movement and the Democratic Party after 9/11*. Cambridge University Press.

Holsti, O. (2011). *American public opinion on the Iraq War*. University of Michigan Press.

Hunt, A. E. (1999). *The turning: A history of Vietnam veterans against the war*. New York University Press.

Hutto, J. (2008). *Antiwar soldier: How to dissent within the ranks of the military*. Nation Books.

Jeralyn. (2008, May 27). Caucuses vs. primaries: A report. *Talk Left: The Politics of Crime*. www.talkleft.com/story/2008/5/27/92144/7994/elections2008/Caucuses-vs-Primaries-A-Report-.

Johnson, H. & Wilson, G. C. (1972). Army in anguish. *The Washington Post*. Pocket Books.

Joseph, P. (1987). *Cracks in the Empire: State Politics in the Vietnam War*. Columbia University Press.

Kahl, C. (2014, June 15). No, Obama didn't lose Iraq. *Politico Magazine*. www.politico.com/magazine/story/2014/06/no-obama-didnt-lose-iraq-107874/.

Karpf, D. (2012). *The MoveOn effect: The unexpected transformation of American political advocacy*. Oxford University Press.

Kennan, G. F. (1983, May). The bishops' letter. *New York Times*. www.nytimes.com/1983/05/01/opinion/the-bishops-letter.html.

Kershner, S. (2023). "A constant surveillance" the New York State Police and the student peace movement, 1965–1973. *The Global Sixties, 16*(1), 22–52. www.tandfonline.com/doi/abs/10.1080/27708888.2023.2165781.

Kimball, D. (2023, September). Defending the de facto nuclear test ban. *Arms Control Today*. www.armscontrol.org/act/2023-09/focus/defending-de-facto-nuclear-test-ban.

Kissinger, H. (1979). *The White House years*. Little, Brown.

Kissinger, H. (2003). *Ending the Vietnam War: A history of America's involvement in and extraction from the Vietnam War*. Simon and Schuster.

Knickerbocker, B. (2007, January 19). Whither all the war protesters? *Christian Science Monitor*. www.csmonitor.com/2007/0119/p01s03-ussc.html.

Knopf, J. W. (1998). *Domestic society and international cooperation: The impact of protest on US arms control policy*. Cambridge University Press.

Koncewicz, M. (2024). The Vietnam moratorium and the limits of Cold War congressional peace politics. In D. Bessner and M. Brenes (Eds.), *Rethinking U.S. world power: Domestic histories of U.S. foreign relations* (pp. 185–208). Palgrave Macmillan.

Kull, S., Ramsay, C. & Lewis, E. (2003/2004). Misperceptions, the media, and the Iraq War. *Political Science Quarterly, 118*(4), 569–598. www.jstor.org/stable/30035697.

Lepre, G. (2011). *Fragging: Why US soldiers assaulted their officers in Vietnam*. Texas Tech University Press.

Lutz, M. (2009, March 29). *The social pulpit: Barack Obama's social media toolkit*. Edelman. https://issuu.com/edelman_pr/docs/social_pulpit__barack_obamas_social_media_toolkit/12.

Maar, H. R.III. (2021). *Freeze! The grassroots movement to halt the arms race and end the Cold War*. Cornell University Press.

Mazarr, M. (2019). *Leap of faith: Hubris, negligence, and America's greatest foreign policy tragedy*. PublicAffairs.

McAdam, D., & Tarrow, S. G. (2010). Ballots and barricades: On the reciprocal relationship between elections and social movements. *Perspectives on Politics, 8*(2), 529–542. https://doi.org/10.1017/S1537592710001234.

McWethy, J. (1972). *The power of the Pentagon*. Congressional Quarterly.

Meyer, D. S., & Corrigall-Brown, C. (2005). Coalitions and political context: U.S. movements against wars in Iraq. *Mobilization: An International Journal, 10*(3), 327–344. https://doi.org/10.17813/maiq.10.3.f8u6t4u2708kw442.

Moore, D. (2002, August 23). Majority of Americans favor attacking Iraq to oust Saddam Hussein. *Gallup News*. https://news.gallup.com/poll/6658/majority-americans-favor-attacking-iraq-oust-saddam-hussein.aspx.

Morton, T. [Presenter]. (2006, May 28). The Vietnam War and Richard Nixon's secret nuclear alert. (Episode 3) [Radio broadcast episode]. In *Torn Curtain*. ABC Radio National. www.abc.net.au/listen/programs/specialbroadcasts/vietnam-war-and-richard-nixons-secret-nuclear-alert/11807120.

Moser, B. (2006). Virginia's rumbling rebels. *The Nation*. October 26, 2006. www.thenation.com/article/archive/virginias-rumbling-rebels/.

Moser, R. (1996). *The new winter soldiers: GI and veteran dissent during the Vietnam era*. Rutgers University Press.

Moyer, B., McAllister, J., Finley, M., & Soifer, S. (2001). *Doing democracy: The MAP model for organizing social movements*. New Society.

Naval History and Heritage Command (1973). Report by the Special Subcommittee on Disciplinary Problems in the US Navy. U.S. Congress. House. Committee on Armed Forces. Report by the Special Subcommittee on Disciplinary Problems in the US Navy. 92nd Cong., 2d sess., 1973, H.A.S.C. 92–81. Washington, DC: Government Printing Office, 1973. www.history .navy.mil/research/library/online-reading-room/title-list-alphabetically/r/ report-by-special-subcommittee-disciplinary-problems-us-navy.html.

Nixon, R. (1978). *RN: The memoirs of Richard Nixon*. Grosset & Dunlap.

Nuclear Threat Initiative. (n.d.). NTI launches "make nukes history" campaign to spotlight nuclear weapons risks ahead of academy awards. www.nti.org/ news/nuclear-threat-initiative-launches-make-nukes-history-campaign-to-spotlight-nuclear-weapon-risks-ahead-of-academy-awards/.

Obama, B. (2020). *Promised Land*. Penguin Random House.

O'Hanlon, M. (2005, January 1). Iraq without a plan. *Brookings Institution*.

O'Sullivan, S. (2019, May 9). A Watergate burglar's account of his crimes – and what it tells us about the Mueller probe. *The Washington Post*. www.washing tonpost.com/outlook/2019/05/09/watergate-burglars-account-his-crimes-and-what-it-tells-us-about-mueller-indictments/.

Overy, R. (2024, June 23). Why it's too late to stop World War III. *The Telegraph*. www.telegraph.co.uk/books/authors/world-war-three-too-late-history-violence/.

Parsons, D. L. (2017). *Dangerous grounds: Antiwar coffeehouses and military dissent in the Vietnam era*. University of North Carolina Press.

Pew Global Attitudes Project. (2003, March 18). *America's image further erodes, Europeans want weaker ties: A nine-country survey*. The Pew Research Center for the People & the Press. www.pewresearch.org/wp-content/uploads/sites/2/pdf/175.pdf.

President's Commission on an all-volunteer armed force. (1970, February). *The report of the President's Commission on an all-volunteer armed force*. Collier-McMillan. https://archive.org/details/reportofpresiden1970unse.

Prochnau, B. (1981, May 6). Mormon Church joins opposition to MX program. *The Washington Post*. www.washingtonpost.com/archive/politics/1981/05/ 06/mormon-church-joins-opposition-to-mx-program/d1402f0c-b9aa-435e-8c91-499d43bdf9a2/.

Reich, K. (1997, June 23). The bloody march that shook L.A. *Los Angeles Times*. www.latimes.com/archives/la-xpm-1997-06-23-mn-6188-story.html.

Ricks, T. E. (2006). *Fiasco: The American military adventure in Iraq, 2003 to 2005*. Penguin Books.

Riedel, B. (2021, September 11). 9/11 and Iraq: The making of a tragedy. *Lawfare*.

Robinson, J. (2023, March 29). American experience: The movement and the "madman." *KPBS*. www.kpbs.org/news/2023/03/24/american-experience-the-movement-and-the-madman.

Rose, T. (2022, December 12). America's nuclear sponge: Opposition to militarization in Nevada. *American Historical Association*. www.historians.org/research-and-publications/perspectives-on-history/december-2022/americas-nuclear-sponge-opposition-to-militarization-in-nevada.

Rumsfeld, D. (2012). *Known and unknown: A memoir*. Sentinel.

Sagan, S. & Suri, J. (2003). The madman nuclear alert. *International Security 27* (4), 150–183.

Savitsky, Z. (2022, August 15). Nuclear war could cause years long global famine. *Science*. www.science.org/content/article/nuclear-war-would-cause-yearslong-global-famine.

Schell, J. (2007). *The seventh decade: The new shape of nuclear danger*. Metropolitan Books.

Scoles, S. (2023, December 1). Behind the scenes at a U.S. factory building new nuclear bombs. *Scientific American, 329*(5), 39–45. www.scientificamerican.com/article/behind-the-scenes-at-a-u-s-factory-building-new-nuclear-bombs/.

Sharp, G. (2005). *Waging nonviolent struggle: 20th century practice and 21st century potential*. Porter Sargent.

Singer, P. (2013, September 1). Opposition to Syria attack emerges in Congress. *USA Today*. www.usatoday.com/story/news/politics/2013/09/01/congress-syria-rand-paul-kerry/2752965/.

Small, M. (2010, June). Bring the boys home now! Antiwar activism and withdrawal from Vietnam – and Iraq. *Diplomatic History 34*(3), 543–553. www.jstor.org/stable/24915900.

Small, M. (1988). *Johnson, Nixon, and the doves*. Rutgers University Press.

Smith, R. M. (1970, September 2). Vote in Senate. *The New York Times*. www.nytimes.com/1970/09/02/archives/vote-in-senate.html.

Solnit, R. (2005, June 14). Acts of hope: Challenging empire on the world stage. *Mother Jones*. www.motherjones.com/politics/2005/06/acts-hope-challenging-empire-world-stage/.

Solo, P. (1988). *From protest to policy: Beyond the freeze to common security*. Ballinger.

Sorley, L. (1999). *A better war: The unexamined victories and final tragedy of America's last years in Vietnam*. Harcourt Brace.

Stacewicz, R. (1997). *Winter soldiers: An oral history of the war*. Twayne.

Stanton, S. L. (1985). *The rise and fall of an American Army: U.S. ground forces in Vietnam, 1965–1973*. Presidio Press.

Stockholm International Peace Research Institute. (2024). *SIPRI yearbook 2024: Armaments, disarmament and international security.* Oxford University Press.

Strong, J. (2017). *Public opinion, legitimacy and Tony Blair's War in Iraq.* Routledge.

Talbot, S. (Producer and director). (2023, March 28). *The movement and the madman.* PBS. www.pbs.org/wgbh/americanexperience/films/movement-and-madman/.

Talbott, S. (1984). Buildup and breakdown. *Foreign Affairs, 62,* 3, 587–615.

Talbott, S. (1985). *Deadly gambits: The Reagan Administration and nuclear arms control.* Vintage Books.

Tarrow, S. (1998). *Power in Movements: Social Movements and Contentious Politics.* 2nd ed. Cambridge University Press.

Tarrow, S. (2012). *Strangers at the gates: Movements and states in contentious politics.* Cambridge University Press.

Tilly, C. (2004). *Social movements, 1768–2004.* Boulder. Paradigm Press.

Tilly, C. & Tarrow, S.G. (2015). *Contentious politics.* Oxford University Press.

Tollefson, J. (1994, March 1). Conscientious objection to the Vietnam War. *OAH Magazine of History* (3), 75–82. https://doi.org/10.1093/maghis/8.3.75.

Tollefson, J. W. (1990). Draft resistance and evasion. In J. W. Chambers II (Ed.), *The Oxford companion to American military history* (pp. 236–238). Oxford University Press.

Union of Concerned Scientists. (2021, December 16). *Nobel laureates call on Biden to reduce risk of nuclear war, calm arms race with Russia, China.* www.ucsusa.org/about/news/nobel-laureates-call-biden-reduce-nuclear-risk.

United States State Department. (2021, October 5). Fact sheet: Transparency in the U.S. nuclear weapons stockpile. www.state.gov/wp-content/uploads/2021/10/Fact-Sheet_Unclass_2021_final-v2-002.pdf.

UPI. (2008, November 21). Obama raised half-billion online. UPI. www.upi.com/Top_News/2008/11/21/Obama-raised-half-billion-online/30681227273978/.

Van Atta, D. (2008). *With honor: Melvin Laird in war, peace, and politics.* University of Wisconsin Press.

Veith, G. J. (2013). *Black April: The fall of South* Vietnam, 1973–1975. Encounter Books.

Walker, M. (2008). The year of the insurgents: The 2008 US presidential campaign. *International Affairs 84*(6), 1095–1107. https://doi.org/10.1111/j.1468-2346.2008.00759.x.

Waller, D. C. (1987). *Congress and the nuclear freeze.* University of Massachusetts Press.

Wallerstein, I. (2003, July-August). U.S. weakness and the struggle for hegemony. *Monthly Review, 55*(3), 23–29. https://doi.org/10.14452/MR-055-03-2003-07_3.

Wells, T. (1994). *The war within: America's battle over Vietnam.* University of California Press.

The White House. (2022, January 3). *Joint statement by the leaders of the five nuclear weapons states on preventing nuclear war and avoiding arms races.* www.whitehouse.gov/briefing-room/statements-releases/2022/01/03/p5-statement-on-preventing-nuclear-war-and-avoiding-arms-races/.

The White House. (2022, November 15–17). *G20 Bali leaders' declaration.* www.whitehouse.gov/briefing-room/statements-releases/2022/11/16/g20-bali-leaders-declaration/.

Wittner, L. S. (2003). *Toward nuclear abolition: A history of the world disarmament movement, 1971-present.* Stanford University Press.

Woodward, B. (2004). *Plan of attack: The definitive account of the decision to invade Iraq.* Simon & Schuster.

Yankelovich, D. & Doble, J. (1984, October). The public mood: Nuclear weapons and the USSR. *Foreign Affairs, 63*(1), 33–46. https://doi.org/10.2307/20042083.

Acknowledgments

Many individuals contributed to the creation of this work. I am indebted to Professor David S. Meyer for inviting me to participate in the February 2024 conference "Finding Effective Strategies to Advocate for Peace and Nuclear Security: Mining the Past to Inform the Future" at the University of California at Irvine. That conference was packed with penetrating analyses of antiwar and disarmament activism and sparked my interest in writing a comparative analysis of peace movement effectiveness. Meyer encouraged me to write a longer version of my analysis for the Cambridge University Press Elements series on contentious politics, which he co-edits with Professor Suzanne Staggenborg at the University of Pittsburgh. Meyer and Staggenborg were helpful in guiding me through the writing of the manuscript, responding to the peer review comments and submitting the completed work for publication. Their helpful support and editing assistance made this work possible.

I am especially grateful for the encouragement and support for this project I received from Professor Sidney Tarrow, Professor Emeritus at Cornell University and one of the world's most respected scholars of social movements. I met Tarrow initially in the 2000s when he invited me to make a presentation about the Iraq antiwar movement for his graduate social movements class, based on an early version of what later became my book *A Peaceful Superpower: Lessons from the World's Largest Antiwar Movement* (New Village Press, 2023).

Tarrow was very supportive of my work when I was invited to serve as University Lecturer at Cornell in the fall of 2023 and became a visiting affiliated scholar at the University's Reppy Institute for Peace and Conflict Studies. He attended lectures and presentations and always offered constructive comments. He encouraged me to undertake this work for Cambridge University Press Elements.

As the final manuscript was taking shape Tarrow volunteered to read and offer comments on the manuscript. His edits and suggestions were enormously helpful and made this a better work. I am deeply thankful for his generosity and support for this work.

Many others assisted in this work. I received helpful comments and edits on parts of the manuscript from Carolyn Eisenberg, Jonathan Hutto, Arnold Isaacs, Paul Joseph, Robert Levering, Henry Richard Maar III and John McAuliff. I am grateful to the pioneering scholars and participants of the Iraq, Nuclear Freeze and Vietnam peace movements whose work I consulted frequently in preparing this manuscript: Carolyn Eisenberg, Michael Heaney and Fabio Rojas, the late Tom Hayden, Henry Richard Maar III, David Meyer, Melvin Small, Tom Wells, and Lawrence S. Wittner.

I am thankful to Professor Rebecca Slayton, director of the Reppy Institute, for the institutional support that made my research and writing on this project possible, and to Professor Matthew Evangelista, past director of the Reppy Institute and dear friend and colleague, who has provided constant encouragement and support for my work on this and other projects.

I received support from the Kroc Institute for International Peace Studies at the University of Notre Dame and its Director Asher Kaufmann and Associate Director Juan Flores Ramirez. Kristen Elizabeth Wall provided valuable research and editing support as she has for my other writings. I also benefitted from the institutional support of the Fourth Freedom Forum and its president Alistair Millar.

On a personal note, I acknowledge the support and inspiration for this project and all my writing and activism for peace that I received from Karen A. Jacob, my recently deceased wife and life partner. She encouraged me into her final days to complete this work and to carry on the struggle for peace and justice to which we together devoted our lives. This work is lovingly dedicated to her memory.

Cambridge Elements ≡

Contentious Politics

David S. Meyer

University of California, Irvine

David S. Meyer is Professor of Sociology and Political Science at the University of California, Irvine. He has written extensively on social movements and public policy, mostly in the United States, and is a winner of the John D. McCarthy Award for Lifetime Achievement in the Scholarship of Social Movements and Collective Behavior.

Suzanne Staggenborg

University of Pittsburgh

Suzanne Staggenborg is Professor of Sociology at the University of Pittsburgh. She has studied organizational and political dynamics in a variety of social movements, including the women's movement and the environmental movement, and is a winner of the John D. McCarthy Award for Lifetime Achievement in the Scholarship of Social Movements and Collective Behavior.

About the Series

Cambridge Elements series in Contentious Politics provides an important opportunity to bridge research and communication about the politics of protest across disciplines and between the academy and a broader public. Our focus is on political engagement, disruption, and collective action that extends beyond the boundaries of conventional institutional politics. Social movements, revolutionary campaigns, organized reform efforts, and more or less spontaneous uprisings are the important and interesting developments that animate contemporary politics; we welcome studies and analyses that promote better understanding and dialogue.

Cambridge Elements ☰

Contentious Politics

Elements in the Series

A full series listing is available at: www.cambridge.org/ECTP

For EU product safety concerns, contact us at Calle de José Abascal, 56–1°,
28003 Madrid, Spain or eugpsr@cambridge.org.